We Are The Socks

Lessons Along a
Peacemaker's Journey

Daniel L. Buttry

Read The Spirit Books
an imprint of
David Crumm Media, LLC
Canton, Michigan

For more information and further discussion, visit
InterfaithPeacemakers.com

Cover art and design by
Rick Nease
www.RickNeaseArt.com

Geographic Table of Contents
by Cody Harrell

Published By
Read The Spirit Books
an imprint of
David Crumm Media, LLC
42015 Ford Rd., Suite 234
Canton, Michigan, USA

For information about customized editions, bulk purchases
or permissions, contact David Crumm Media, LLC at info@
DavidCrummMedia.com

This book is dedicated to
the rising generation of peacemakers;
especially to:
Lance, Christina, Pini,
Philip, Phillip, Boaz,
Michelline, Fabrice,
Wado, Jabbie, Asher,
Henna, Feraz, Manal,
Iana, Alexander, Keti,
and many others.

May you be fruitful
and multiply!

You are the Socks!

Contents

Acknowledgments

Every book is a community project, and I am grateful to all who had a hand in this particular endeavor.

I am grateful to my wife, Sharon, for her companionship, collaboration, creativity and courage. We've shared many of these adventures together as well as the encompassing adventure of our marriage and ministry. We actually make a great matched pair of socks.

Working again with *Read The Spirit*, publisher of three of my earlier books, has been a joy. David Crumm is one of the greatest encouragers I've ever met. I think he believes in what I do far more than I do! John Hile is always doing the deep background work—I really don't know what he is doing, but I see his fingerprints everywhere in the process. Becky Hile has been a joy to work with both in editing the Interfaith Peacemakers Department of *Read The Spirit's* website and in the photos for this book. Dmitri Barvinok brought passion and skill to the overall editing, and Celeste Dykas did the copy editing, bringing ideas that have enhanced the book. Thanks to artist Rick Nease who engaged spiritually with the manuscript as the inspiration for the cover art. I deeply appreciate dear friends and peacemaking colleagues Ken Sehested, Molly Marshall and David LaMotte for their contributions to the book and their gracious engagement not only with this project but in our shared peacemaking journeys.

International Ministries called me to full-time service as a peacemaking missionary. They have encouraged and supported me, particularly Reid Trulson, Charles Jones and Ben Chan. Each has been amazingly supportive as my leader over the years. So many other staff and colleagues at International Ministries, some based around the world, have been wonderful partners in faith, hope and love.

I also deeply appreciate the many people and congregations who have given to support my peacemaking mission work. I couldn't get to any of these places on my own. In every case, there was a generous community behind me holding me up with their finances and prayers. These are their stories, too.

Then there are the generations. The older peacemakers blazed the trail for others and me. We've had role models to look up to, encouragers to enable us to press on our way and teachers to refine our passions with skills and competency. There are my peers, my companions in the struggle. We've shared so much together, seen some great victories and cried together over disheartening losses.

Last is the rising generation, some of whose members I've been privileged to train and to whom I dedicate this book. My socks are getting pretty ratty. I often check them when I know I'll have to go through airport security and take off my shoes—I don't want my toes poking through! There comes a time when old socks need to be thrown out. My time will come to be set aside. Already I can see some beautiful pairs of socks about the work of covering the world's wounds. So I'm ready... but I do like these socks that I am. Maybe I'll put them on for a peace journey yet one more time.

Foreword

I first met Dan Buttry in the basement of a Baptist church in Raleigh, North Carolina, where he was leading a peacemaking workshop. I was working for the North Carolina Council of Churches at the time, as their Associate for Peace. I had heard good things about Dan and wanted to see what he had to say.

I was immediately intrigued by Dan and his work, but I confess that I had to take it in slowly. Meeting Dan Buttry for the first time, it would be forgivable to be a bit skeptical of this tall, thin, engaging, energetic man, with his easy laughter and bright eyes. He leans forward instinctively, smiles almost constantly, listens closely, and shares encouraging stories of peace breaking out in the most unlikely times and places. How could he be speaking to issues of deep conflict, yet be so joyful? Does he not know how violent and hateful the world really is?

We live in a time when cynicism is often equated with realism, and hope is frequently considered to be fundamentally naive. Because the world is a cruel and difficult place, according to this worldview, those who believe in other ways of living must be dangerously out of touch with reality. As hard as I fight against that narrative, my culture is soaked in it, and sometimes it leaks in.

Reading these pages, however, it is almost impossible to escape the conclusion that Dan has directly encountered much more of that cruelty, hatred and injustice than most people ever will. He has chosen to keep engaging—over and over—because, while he sees these painful realities with honest clarity, he has also been a part of transformational reconciliation—over and over.

As Dan so compellingly shows us, there is more than one kind of hope. Yes, there is naive hope, based on inexperience with hard realities, but there is also a thicker, richer hope that is born of knowing those hard realities intimately, and experiencing the light that can shine in those dark places. Along with the capacity for astounding viciousness, human beings have the capacity to remember our own humanity and each other's.

Yes, human beings can be unspeakably cruel, and we can also be extraordinarily courageous, vulnerable, and Spirit-led. Perhaps most amazingly, we have a deep capacity for healing and being healed. That which is broken need not remain broken, and we can employ our healing skills more often and more deftly with the help of experienced guides and teachers like Dan.

In this book, Dan shares stories of people summoning the courage to get uncomfortable, to risk, to forgive, to discern each other's humanity through the fog of long-held enmity, bigotry and undeniably legitimate reasons not to trust each other. Those stories are both inspiring and instructional, giving us templates for how we might reimagine our own relationships and social structures.

He also tells stories of things not going so well, of times when people didn't quite rise to the challenge, and moments when he didn't know what to do. A friend of mine once counseled me to be wary of those whose stories always feature themselves in the role of the hero. Though Dan does sometimes teach through stories where he was given the right words to say or the elicitive exercise that was needed in a given moment, he also writes of being baffled by how to respond to an angry workshop participant, treading water while his co-facilitator strategized, and being humbled by the wisdom and creativity of parties to conflicts, who took things in directions he didn't anticipate, and which were better than he could design. He writes of his own struggles and reversals of understanding, notably in the story that gives this book its name. Dan's humility makes these stories accessible, though they happen in many lands and in situations I may never encounter.

I am also grateful for Dan's clear admission that there are not always happy endings. He is not making an argument for a foolproof conflict transformation formula, but that by showing up, by risking, by studying conflict transformation techniques and developing peacemaking skills, by humbly asking for God's guidance and following it when it is offered (sometimes against our better judgement!), we can make space for the Spirit to move, and miraculous reconciliations really can come to pass. The peace that Dan points to in this book is not undisturbed tranquility; it is not uncomplicated or easily achieved. It is not always gentle. Just as there is more than one kind of hope, however, there is more than one kind of peace. The kind that Dan is working for and teaching is not placidity, or lack of struggle. It is not conflict avoidance. It is not the cheap peace that comes from ignoring injustice or protecting oneself from difficulty. Dan's version of peacemaking involves stepping toward conflict rather than away from it, courageously confronting injustice rather than concealing it, engaging with those who seem to be our enemies in dignity and love, and with creativity, rather than meeting violence with violence and hatred with hatred. This is shalom, nourishing justice and right relationships. This is what it means to be 'repairers of the breach and restorers of streets to live in.'

What Dan is proposing here, and has given his life to, is radical. He has spent the last several decades experimenting with what happens when we take Jesus seriously in situations of conflict. What happens if we define faith by radical inclusion rather than careful exclusion? What happens when we really do love our enemies and pray for those who persecute us?

After meeting Dan in that church, I knew I had more to learn from this man, so I attended a training he taught with his colleague Daniel Hunter in Detroit. Later, Dan invited me to co-facilitate a peacemaker training for nearly two hundred Zambian church leaders in Lusaka. Each time I have been with Dan, I have continued to learn from him. I rejoice that you, holding this book in your hands, now have that opportunity as well.

—David LaMotte

David LaMotte is a singer/songwriter, author, and speaker. His books include *White Flour*, the true story of a whimsical transforming initiative in the face of a 2007 KKK rally, and his most recent offering, *Worldchanging 101: Challenging the Myth of Powerlessness*. He lives in Black Mountain, North Carolina with his wife and son.

Preface

Part reflection and part spiritual memoir, Dan Buttry offers a compelling montage of his global work in peacemaking through this accessible book, *We Are the Socks*. Vignette after vignette tells the story of his ministry all around the world as he has striven to train people in the practice of conflict resolution for the prospect of peace. *Socks* provides the sustained metaphor for the work of covering the wounded "feet" through compassionate action.

As a theological educator, I especially appreciated his use of Scripture to engage suffering communities. Biblical stories such as Jesus weeping over Jerusalem or the widow Rizpah who loses two sons to war connect with the lament of present day persons who long for cessation of violence in their land. His skillful movement from an ancient context to the urgent needs of the present allows the power of Scripture to evoke repentance and healing.

Dr. Buttry employs creative pedagogy in his training; he gets people moving, and they embody the characters in conflict and discover nonviolent means of responding. He knows that lecturing is not enough; for peace depends upon forming new patterns of relationship, and he is adept at prompting these. Peacemaking can come from playing games, also, and he cites an experience where the conversation between two conflicting tribes was going nowhere until after they played a game of soccer/futbol.

Of particular interest to me as President of Central Baptist Theological Seminary is his recounting of his work in Kenya in 2011 alongside Wilson Gathungu, our alumnus, who has clearly found his vocation in peacemaking initiatives. A native Kenyan, he well understands the dynamics of tribal conflict and the toll violence has taken on his people. Two of Central's faculty members, Drs. Terry and Ruth Rosell, and their four young adult children worked in collaboration with Dan and Wilson, and they witnessed real breakthroughs where long-standing conflict had ensued.

In recognition of his expansive work, Central awarded Dan the Doctor of Divinity, *honoris causa*, in May 2009. His writing, mission service, and global influence are truly significant, and Central is proud to claim him! He has taught for Central and traveled with us to Myanmar for global immersion experiences.

The focus of his ministry is reiterated through the voices of those on the margins. With them he knows that "you can't just talk peace and reconciliation, you have to do it!" He writes, "Change seldom comes from the top down in ways that empower or support the margins. Almost always, change happens because the margins find a way to speak out and stand for their needs and their rights" (p. 88).

I shared this perceptive book with a ministry colleague, Seth Vopat, who observed: "Daniel Buttry is to peacemaking what Wendell Berry is to local farm and rural life. Through Buttry's stories, really a recounting of his life's work, we cannot walk away believing peace is simply a nice ideal Jesus liked to talk about. Buttry encourages us to risk so that we might hear the voices who cry out in the midst of lands scarred by the horrors of war."

Buttry closes the book by mentioning that he has met and seen several new bright socks going out into the world. Indeed, he dedicates the text to young peacemakers that he has been mentoring. Some of our Central students have received his training, and they attest to the significant impact he has had on their lives. Though Dan describes his own socks are getting old and ratty, perhaps they have many more journeys in the service of peace in them.

—*Molly T. Marshall*

Molly T. Marshall is President and Professor of Theology and Spiritual Formation at Central Baptist Theological Seminary in Shawnee, Kansas. Theological education is her life's work, and she has the privilege of witnessing God's formative work in the lives of students. A theologian and writer, she is widely published and lectures internationally.

Introduction

"If you want to build a ship, don't drum up people together to collect wood and assign them tasks and work, but rather teach them to long for the endless immensity of the sea."

—Antoine de Saint-Exupery

What Dan Buttry does in *We Are the Socks* is what he does better than anyone I know: Write vivid, easy-to-read narratives that are hopeful but not sentimental, honest but not cynical, revealing without being voyeuristic, personal without being self-serving, sometimes humorous but never silly. And the people he writes about, in these few selected episodes out of literally dozens of others from his global work, are not drawn from self-selected elites—the morally heroic or intelligent or ingenious. Mostly they are commonplace folk, drawn from every sort of circumstance, typical admixtures of hope and doubt, compassion and malice, vision and blind sightedness. Not your stereotypical candidates for sainthood. In other words, folk like us, like the ones in our churches and neighborhoods and families.

What distinguishes the characters in this book is, first, they have experienced the blunt force of repression of one sort or another; and, second, they hold out hope for miracles, for the things that make for peace.

Not miracles in the manner of Cecil B. DeMille mov-
ie-marvels or Stephen Spielberg special effects. And not
miracles in the sense of abrogating the laws of nature. Miracles
in the sense of utter surprise, of the completely unexpected,
the hardly imaginable, coming to pass—joyously so, for those
of low estate; horrifyingly so, for the high riders. The awe
required for miracle-minders is the expectation that one day,
in one form or another, the sum of our work will be greater
than the parts. It will arrive, seemingly, out of nowhere. As the
Prophets often noted, a way will emerge from no-way.

"Peacemaking is not a matter of social engineering," Dan
writes, nor is it "a technique to be practiced," but is "an art in
which turning points come through some action and words
spoken that are completely unplanned."

This reminds me of an experience my wife had in her work
as a maximum-security prison chaplain. One of her weekly
duties was to accompany the Native American group outside for their prayer circle and passing the sacred pipe. (In a
tobacco-free institution, this particular religious affiliation had
become a popular choice.) On one occasion two of the men
had sat outside the circle, talking, as the ceremony progressed.
Afterward, Nancy pulled them aside as the group returned
to their cell blocks, quietly reminding them that, first, their
behavior was disrespectful and, two, that it was against prison
policy (aimed at reducing coordinated gang activity).

Juan went off, enraged, yelling and threatening. Some of the
inmates heard and came back, making counter threats. The
escalating rage stopped just short of a riot. (It doesn't take
much to reach a boiling point in prison, full as it is of daily
humiliations that accumulate like metal shavings to a magnet.)

Afterward, Nancy called Juan to her office. He arrived face
still flushed with vindictiveness, ready for a confrontation.
Without pause, Nancy asked him, "Juan, what is your favorite
song?"

"Huh?" he asked, not from lack of hearing but from surprise. So Nancy simply repeated the question. "What's your favorite song?"

The look on his face was incredulous, but he managed to say, "'Imagine' by John Lennon."

Now it was Nancy's turn to be surprised, but that didn't slow her. She immediately got on her computer and called up a YouTube recording of the song and hit "play."

What happened next was a three-minute transformation of biblical proportions, all because of the improvisational skills of a conflict transformer (of diminutive size) who took a surprising initiative to counter "the realism of resignation to violence" (as Dan describes the work of one of his co-trainers, Boaz Keibarak, during a workshop in a conflicted area of Kenya).

"History, despite its wrenching pain, cannot be unlived," the poet Maya Angelou wrote, "but if faced with courage [and imagination!], need not be lived again."

In my decades of work starting and sustaining faith-based peace and justice organizations, I was occasionally approached by students wanting advice on how to take on this sort of career. I learned over the years to be blunt, saying that three-fourths of the work I did was not unlike what any small nonprofit administrator has to do: manage volunteers, craft and implement appropriate financial development strategies and project planning, maintain accountability structures, sustain communication tools.

In other words, much peacemaking work is thoroughly unglamorous. And measureable success is hard to come by. The successes are often fragile and subject to cracks, even collapse. For instance, the mediation work among the Nagas of Northeast India, which Dan mentions in this work, is in its 20th year and still far short of the hoped-for transformation. Luckily, in that region are people who practice what German theologian Dorothee Sölle called "revolutionary patience," a kind of patience that is not passive, that remains expectant amid the lulls of productive activity, that knows the engines of change can also run in reverse, that is not overly wrought when hopeful breakthroughs stall not far out of the gate, that is not so distracted by the lack of progress that they keep their eyes and ears alert to some moment of leverage easily over-looked amid the routine headlines and day-to-day tedium.

Or, to switch metaphors, what is needed to sustain effective social change is what the Brazilian theological movement of the late '60s and early '70s, in the context of a brutal military dictatorship, articulated as *permanente firmeza*, roughly trans-lated as "relentless firmness (or resolve)." Whether referencing an explicit religious orientation or not, this characteristic can only be sustained by a vision of the future that does not sit waiting for us to arrive but is actively pushing its way through the crowded onslaught of history in our direction. Only those touched by this beatific vision know the truth of what Walter Brueggemann notes: "The empire always wants to limit what is *possible* to what is *available*." Peacemakers are those forged in the fiery vision that "what is promised is more than what is possessed" (Brueggemann).

Effective peacemakers are by necessity a durable lot, with scars—emotional and sometimes physical—as verifiable evi-dence of having counted the cost. Those on the Way of Jesus know the secret of success pulses in this line from the writer of Hebrews who wrote that Jesus, "for the sake of the joy that was set before him, endured the cross" (12:2). There is a saying in the Philippines, "Those who would give light must endure burning." Being soaked in this joy is the only way to endure the flames of defeat, desertion, betrayal, and despair.

To create an effective movement for redemptive engage-ment, reflective work must be integrated with affective learning in the context of a community of conviction. Mind and imagination must be addressed, and these must be tethered to disciplines of concrete and communal commitments.

But, of course, the peace that must be made is not always way over yonder. (Dan deals with this in the "Where's Our Chicken?" chapter.) The bloodless violence we commit in much more pedestrian and familiar relations is different in scale but not in substance from the enmity that sparks war. My vote for the most blistering text in the Newer Testament comes from James:

> *"How great a forest is set ablaze by a small fire! And the tongue is a fire. The tongue is placed among our members as a world of iniquity; it stains the whole body, sets on fire the cycle of nature, and is itself set on fire by hell. For every species of beast and bird, of reptile and sea creature, can be tamed, but no one can tame the tongue—a restless evil, full of deadly poison" (vv. 5b-8).*

The most intimidating piece of peacemaking work I've undertaken wasn't in a war zone. It was in my own home.

It was late. I was tired. I'd not come near finishing urgent work prior to leaving town. I didn't start packing a suitcase until midnight preparing for a pre-dawn flight. Nancy was up late, too, and similarly preoccupied and stressed. Something came up. I honestly don't remember what. In a few short words we found ourselves pinching each other's emotional sciatic nerves. We went to bed with our backs to each other.

A few hours later I was in a state of deep unrest sitting in the airport waiting to board—knowing what I needed to do but dreading it more than a root canal. But finally I did. I went to a nearby pay phone [see Wikipedia for definition], dropped in a quarter, dialed our number and heard Nancy's voice.

"I'm sorry for last night," I said.

"Me, too," came the response.

We didn't talk long. We didn't analyze the conflict. We just raised affection-laced truce flags, implicitly admitting that the channel connecting our lives needed dredging. Acknowledging the murky water was the key to repairing the flow.

I'm not suggesting that strategies for maintaining a good marriage are similar to negotiating a nuclear arms treaty with Iran. And there are a host of conflicts between these spectral poles needing attention, all of them requiring customized analyses and creative engagements.

What each shares with the others is the requirement of risk, a risk powered by a realism admitting the possibility of miracle, plus the kind of fidelity that sustains patience in the face of seemingly impossible odds. John Paul Lederach, considered the pioneer of conflict transformation theory and practice, urges us to mobilize "moral imagination as the capacity to imagine something rooted in the challenges of the real world yet capable of giving birth to that which does not yet exist."

The future is not fated. Another world is possible.

—Ken Sehested

Rev. Ken Sehested is the author and editor of prayerandpolitiks.org, an online journal at the intersection of spiritual formation and prophetic action. His recent books include two volumes of poetry, *In the Land of the Living: Prayers personal and public* and *In the Land of the Living: Litanies, poems, prayers, and benedictions,* and *Peace Primer II: Quotes from Jewish, Christian and Islamic Scripture & Tradition* (co-edited with Rabbi Lynn Gottlieb and Muslim scholar Rabia Terri Harris).

A Geographic Table of Contents

Middle East

North America

Western Hemisphere

🏠 Home: Hamtramck, Michigan, USA

North America	Latin America & Carribean
1 United States Pages 2, 7, 10, 14, 56, 131	**2** Jamaica Page 140 **3** Bolivia Page 102 **4** Chile Page 107

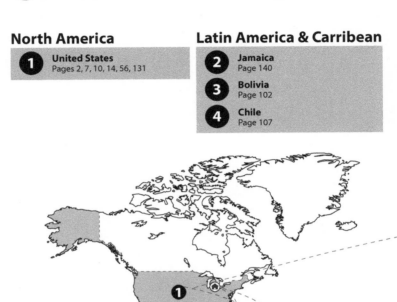

Eastern Hemisphere

Asia

5 Kyrgyzstan
Page 64

6 India
Pages 127, 135, 119

7 Myanmar
Page 98

8 Hong Kong
Page 149

9 Phillipines
Pages XXVII, 10

Middle East

22 Lebanon
Page 59

23 Israel
Page 40

Africa

10 Sierra Leone
Page 123

11 Liberia
Page 2, 7

12 Congo
Pages 10, 40

13 Uganda
Pages 14, 148

14 Ethiopia
Page 67

15 Kenya
Pages 18, 22, 26, 30, 35, 94

Europe

15 Italy
Page 91

16 Croatia
Pages 45, 67

17 Bosnia
Pages 45, 51

18 Serbia
Page 56

19 Poland
Page 111

20 Soviet Union
Page 10

21 Georgia
Pages 72, 77, 81, 84

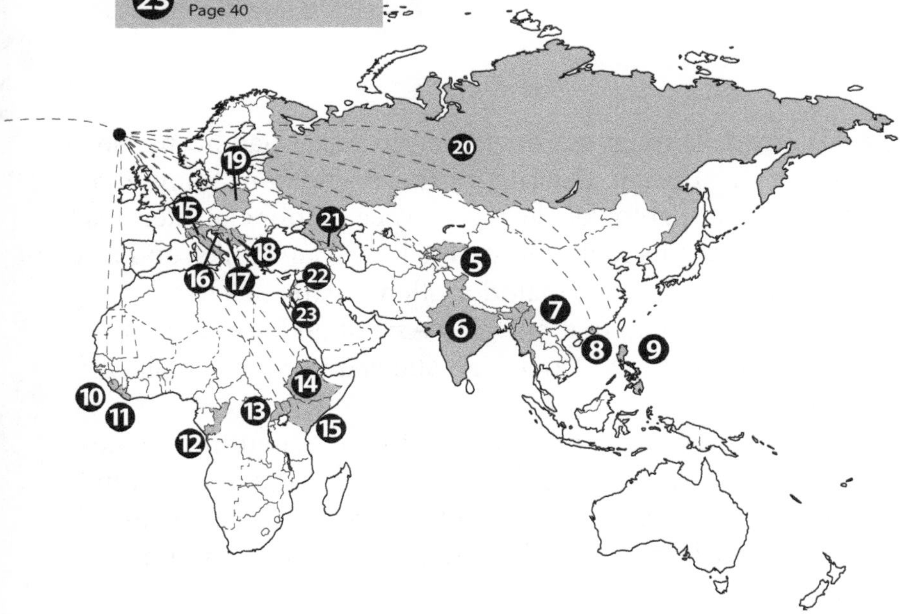

Smells Like Hell

I was trapped. Throughout my travels in Asia I had been able to avoid trying durian. Durian, for those who don't know, is a notorious fruit that looks like a prickly cantaloupe on steroids. The problem isn't its looks but its smell. Durian stinks, and it stinks with an aggressive malodor offensive to your nasal passages. It stinks so bad that hotels in Asia often have signs at the front desk that say, "No durian allowed in rooms, halls or elevators!"

But some people like durian, even love it. Laughing, friends would tell me, "Yes, it smells like hell, but it tastes like heaven!" I found that difficult to believe, so I just made sure to avoid any situation where I might have to give it a try. For years I was successful.

But now I was trapped. I was in the Philippines sitting at a restaurant table with Sharon and a small group of Filipino friends. Fred wanted to have durian with our meal. When I tried to dissuade him, Fred repeated that old saying with a big smile, "It smells like hell but taste like heaven." Sharon refused to give it a try, leaving me as the sole missionary from the U.S. to join our Filipino friends in their delightful feast. There was no gracious way out of this predicament. You could say I bit the bullet, but this was worse.

When the durian was cut open I almost gagged. How does one describe the smell of this fruit? I'm not Dante, so my description of the hellish odor will lack poetic depth. (I hope, dear reader, you are not reading this while eating. If so I urge you to put the book down immediately or skip to another chapter.) Ready? The most accurate description I can give of the smell of durian is a combination of fresh vomit and old junior high gym clothes that have been forgotten for months in a locker. The smell isn't the only problem. The texture is revolting as well—a mass of yellow-orange goo that looks and feels as rotten as it smells.

I now know what it feels like to star on "Fear Factor." I smiled, dipped my hand into the messy guts of the durian, grabbed a wad and shoved it in my mouth. I waited in vain for the heavenly taste. I now knew with awful intensity that durian tastes like hell, too. I swallowed it quickly as

Fred relishes his durian.

my Filipino "friends" laughed heartily. They were proud of me for making such a game effort.

Durian smells like hell, but it really isn't of hell. God made durian. Don't ask me why. That is a mystery along with mosquitos. But a lot of people in Asia love durian. Again, don't ask me why.

But there are many other things that smell like hell and are truly emanations coming from the pit of evil. In the Philippines and so many places I've visited, I have worked with the consequences of war and violence. I've stood amid shattered homes, seen bombed-out apartments that still may have bodies inside. I've slept in refugee camps and seen disfigured bodies of those whose limbs have been playfully hacked off by drugged-out child soldiers. General William Tecumseh Sherman said during the U.S. Civil War as he oversaw the scorched earth devastation of his march through the South, "War is hell." Maybe not exactly, but it sure smells like it. When you see the lost lives, the disfigured bodies, the torn families, the shattered communities and the scarred earth, this sure smells like hell. When you see the greed, drive for profit and lust for power that runs so much ruin, it sure smells like hell.

I've seen the levels of hell in human trafficking. Many of my missionary colleagues work in an effort to halt human trafficking and in programs to alleviate the damage done in lives of the victims of sex trades, many of them children. Human trafficking smells like hell.

I've seen the misery that can come from poverty up close. I've seen it in inner cities in which I've lived. I've seen it in the slums of Calcutta (now Kolkata) and Manila and Lagos and Addis Ababa. I've seen people living in shipping containers. I've seen children sleeping on the streets covered in rags. I've

Author takes a bit of that hellish-smelling durian.

seen families living in apartments with one bare mattress on the floor to sleep everyone. Poverty smells like hell.

Jesus said in John 10, *"The thief comes only to steal and kill and destroy."* War, human trafficking, poverty, racism, and a host of other evils take away the abundant life that God desires for all God's children. It's a smell God doesn't like.

When it smells bad, we bring out the air freshener. That's our job, to be the air freshener in the world where it smells like hell. The Bible says in 1 John 3, *"The Son of God was revealed for this purpose, to destroy the works of the devil."* So where war and all the various hellish evils grind down human beings, we are to be about the work of undoing those evils. Where there is injustice, we are to do justice. Where there is bondage, we are to bring liberation. Where there is despair, we are to be lights of hope. Where there is prejudice, we are to bring dignity. Like the *Prayer of St. Francis*, it's simply destroying the works of the devil, or overcoming evil with good.

To put another way, where it smells like hell we are to bring the aroma of heaven. The apostle Paul said in 2 Corinthians 2 about how God in Christ *"through us spreads in every place the fragrance that comes from knowing him. For we are the aroma of Christ. ... "* We are to be the smell of heaven, the aroma of life where it smells of death.

God willing, I'll never have to eat durian again! But I know I'll smell that pungent stench of hell again and again in this world. That smell is my call to be faithful, not to gag on what is ugly and run away. The smell is my call to pray and engage. It's the call to be the overpowering

More?!

and life-giving aroma of grace, mercy and hope. It's the call to be the fragrance of God, the smell of heaven.

This book is about the smells of hell and the fragrance of heaven worked out in ordinary people. Sometimes, the air freshener of goodness and God pops up in surprising places and from people you might least expect to bring that breath of fresh air. Along the way, as a trainer in peacemaking and conflict transformation, I taught people some lessons, but I also learned far more lessons myself. I invite you to come along on part of the journey with me. Perhaps you will learn some lessons that will release the aroma of grace and peace in you more intensely.

PART 1

Socks Saga

So how does a book about peace have "socks" in the title? A strange tale, but one that needs to be told.

CHAPTER 1

Pack Extra Socks

I WAS IN my pre-trip routine: counting out the number of days I'd be away, then counting out the various clothes I'd need. Shirts, handkerchiefs, underwear, socks. *Pack extra socks to give away.*

It wasn't an audible message, but it was very clear. It was sort of like a visual image of red digital message board scrolling along: *Pack extra socks to give away.* I'd been traveling for over 20 years and had never had any "messages" come my way while packing except for Sharon occasionally giving me a reminder. But nothing like this. And such a strange message: *Pack extra socks to give away.*

I do believe that God speaks to us. I believe God speaks to us through the writings of the Bible. I believe God speaks to our hearts in the middle of worship experiences. I believe God speaks to us through the wise counsel of others. I believe even in moments when God speaks prophetically through people in a "thus says the Lord" moment—though I've also seen that abused by people who claimed to speak for God but couldn't endure a cross-check with other people of spiritual integrity.

But I'd never encountered any story of divine intervention into how a suitcase should be packed. I've never encountered any particular divine concern about socks. *Pack extra socks to give away.* There was plenty of room in the duffle, so I tossed in three extra pairs. What did I have to lose except some socks?

I was going to Liberia, my third peacemaking trip to that long-suffering land. My Liberian peacemaking friend Jimmy Diggs had invited me to come and join him for a series of peace and trauma healing workshops. We started in the rural areas of Bomi County along the highway that came into Monrovia from the northwest. That had been one of the major routes for the rebels to advance into the city. There had been much suffering along that road. The workshop was held in the village of Clark-

The old sanctuary of Providence Baptist Church in Monrovia.

stown, which had been completely destroyed in the war. We met in a church whose roof had been ripped off and all its furniture used for firewood. Jimmy and I traveled around each day, training people from many different communities and churches in that area.

Then we moved into the city for another two-day workshop. We met at Providence Baptist Church, the mother church for all of Liberia. Providence is at the center of the city, next to the old historic legislative building and the original presidential mansion—church and state all together, not the proper Baptist approach, but an accurate expression of Liberian history in these buildings.

The workshop was going very well, with participants from about 20 churches in and around the city. During a break, a tall young man came up to talk with me. We got into some deep conversations that continued over lunch. After eating he and I drifted back to the hall where the training was being held. Somewhere in the conversation I starting picking up various threads about his life that my mind began to weave together. He was

Small groups during the workshop at Providence Baptist Church.

a member of Providence. He lived in New Georgia—I knew where New Georgia was, way on the outskirts of Monrovia. Twice a week he made the trip on foot into church, for Sunday and for a midweek intercessors prayer meeting, but that day he'd come particularly for my workshop. I said, "That's a long trip!" Two hours, in fact, one way.

Then he showed me his feet.

He had hard-polished leather shoes, the kind my mother used to put on me as a child when I went to Sunday school and church. These are shoes with no give—merciless shoes. And he had no socks. He took his shoes off and I could see the ring of red open sores around his ankles; sores that, with every step for two hours, had been rubbed by that hard leather. Across his toes I could see more open wounds from where the top of the shoe had bent with each step.

In all my travels nobody had ever showed me their feet before. I instantly knew why I had been given that message: *Pack extra socks to give away.* Here was a young man, one of God's special children, so committed to provide leadership for his church, so committed to learn the things of peace to help heal his country, so committed to pray, that he would walk two hours on painful feet—one way—to get to his church. God saw the incredibly dedicated heart of this young man and knew his pain. And God sent someone from across the ocean to bring some socks to ease those torn feet. I told him about the message to pack extra socks and that I had a special gift to give to him. He was so excited!

Jesus said:

> *Do not worry about your life, what you will eat or what you will drink, or about your body, what you will wear. Is not life more than food, and the body more than clothing? ... Consider the lilies of the field, how they grow; they neither toil or spin, yet I tell you, even Solomon in all his glory was not clothed like one of these. But if God so clothes the grass of the field, which is alive today and tomorrow is thrown into the oven, will he not much more clothe you—you of little faith.*

(Matthew 6:25, 28-30)

I got an intimate and specific demonstration of the loving care of this God for one of God's children. God knows about the sparrow that falls. God knows about the hairs on our head. And God knew about this young man and his sore feet. I had never seen such a demonstration of divine intervention to meet a specific need dramatically turned into an international relief effort, no less!

The next day just happened to be that young man's birthday. He was spending the night in the church for an all-night prayer meeting, so at least he didn't have to go back home with those hard shoes rubbing his open wounds. Meanwhile, I went back with Jimmy to his house that evening. I gathered up the three pairs of socks. I also had some ointment from my traveling first-aid kit and a bunch of bandages. I dug out a peace T-shirt, too.

We had a special divinely commissioned birthday party. I gave him the socks, and we got him well doctored-up before he slipped them over his feet. No longer would he need to take those painful steps as he journeyed to and from his church.

It's so easy for us to struggle with our needs as if we were all alone in this world. Meeting our needs is up to us and is our concern. But the Scriptures tell us that our needs are also God's concern. God cares for us like a tender parent caring for a child. Do you have trust in that care of God for you? Or do you need a dramatic message to open your eyes to the provision of blessings all around you?

CHAPTER 2

You Are the Socks

I TOLD THE story about the socks again and again. I wrote a journal about it and used it in sermons. The story was a great testimony about God's care and provision. Then something started to nag at the corner of my mind. Like a cancerous growth, this thought came from the edges of my consciousness until it dominated all my free thought.

God sent me to Liberia with extra socks to help one young man with sore feet. We're talking about Liberia, a country that was brutalized by a civil war that left some 100,000 people dead and countless more torn and traumatized. About a third of the population

Poster of Liberian children who were separated from parents in the war.

was displaced, driven from their homes by the horrific levels of violence. And God wanted to give socks to one poor guy who would have done better walking barefoot than with those awful shoes?

It seemed that God had lost all sense of proportionality. Jesus said to the scribes and Pharisees, *"You strain out a gnat but swallow a camel!"* (Matthew 23:24). It seemed to me that same accusation could be leveled at God in this case. God was sending a handful of socks to aid one of the worst human-made disasters on the planet. Instead of being blessed by this story, I was now offended. How could God get it so wrong?

I stopped telling the socks story. Instead of being an inspiration the story was now an offense. I kept my conflict with God quiet, but I also kept quiet about what had happened as I was packing for Liberia and about the young man who needed those socks.

Then one Sunday, months later, I was at my home church. We were singing the opening songs of praise. I was standing in a spirit of worship. Liberia could have been a million miles away. Suddenly a message began to scroll through my mind exactly like the first message, as vivid as could be. *You are the socks* was all it said.

I immediately knew exactly what the message meant, and I started to weep. God did know what happened in Liberia and what was still going on. God knew about every death, every rape, every maiming, every moment of hunger, every cry of despair. God knew it all. God felt it all deeply. The point wasn't a few pairs of socks to help out one person with sore feet. The point was that God was calling me and using me to address some of these deeper pains. I was the socks to cover the wounds of war. God sent me to Liberia to meet some of the needs that were so deep and desperate. I was God's provision, even if in a small and partial way, for some of those needs.

There was no pride in hearing this message. Socks are not a particularly notable item of clothing. My socks are usually an embarrassment—smelly and often filled with holes in the toes.

To be called socks was humbling, but the message spoke to me that I had a role to play.

My dresser drawer has many socks in it, so again there was no pride in being called socks. I knew there were many other socks in the Liberia peacemaking drawer. There are my Liberian hosts who were courageous and committed peacemakers. There are the praying Christian and Muslim women led by Leymah Gbowee who used their prayers and nonviolence to force the Liberian civil war to a negotiated settlement. There are people I have never known or heard of who have done heroic work for peace in some of the most trying circumstances imaginable. There are international friends giving of themselves to do the work of building peace.

Then there are all the other peacemakers around the world in conflict after conflict. The global sock drawers have so many of us in them. I am merely one of those pairs of socks. All of us are part of God's answer to the cries of need out of wars and violent conflicts. We are socks, not to sit in a drawer, but to be used. God intends to pull us out to cover some of the hurts and wounds. God knows those hurts and wounds, and we are each called in our own way to be socks.

CHAPTER 3

I've Got the T-shirt

WHEN I COME back from my peacemaking journeys I lug home suitcases full of dirty clothes. One of the first things I do upon arrive home is to start the wash. One time as I folded the clean clothes there was that purple T-shirt. It had "I LOVE ILOILO" boldly emblazoned on it. Memories came flooding back of all the wonderful friends I have in the Philippines. I remembered our training together and the gift they gave me of that T-shirt. They gave me another T-shirt to take home to my wife, Sharon, a much lovelier shirt. I had a great time in Iloilo, and I have the T-shirt to show for it!

On an earlier trip to the Philippines they gave me a T-shirt about Davao City. It's a great looking shirt with all kinds of flora and fauna from Mindanao including the stunning

Author leading a workshop in the Philippines.

crested eagle. But that shirt was given for a special purpose. It has a durian on it. My Filipino friends bought it in teasing memory of me eating durian. Every time I pull that shirt over my head I get a shiver of post-traumatic memory!

T-shirts are our national dress in the U.S. With our love for freedom of expression T-shirts have become the canvas upon which we depict our loves, our loyalties, and our humor in all its sometimes strange and varied expressions. We can chart the events of our lives by our T-shirts, from schools to championships to concerts.

T-shirts have been one of our cultural gifts to the world. I was once at a World Mission Conference when the missionaries and international guests were gathering in their national dress. What should I wear? I chose a funky T-shirt and blue jeans—the gift of my culture to global clothing styles!

Author with his T-shirt and workshop participants.

In 1988, I went to the Soviet Union just as they were going through the tumultuous changes that brought about the fall of Communism. Before we crossed on the ferry from Finland to Estonia, we spent a day in Helsinki. We visited the floating market, and I was drawn to the T-shirt stall. They had a T-shirt with a massive hammer and sickle with bold letters: "KGB." That would look good on the basketball court fighting for a rebound! I especially loved the T-shirt of the Statue of Liberty with the imposed head of Soviet Premier Gorbachev over the word "PERESTROIKA!" I almost bought it then thought, "No, I'll get a genuine Russian T-shirt." That was a mistake. At the time there was no such things as a genuine Russian T-shirt. The cotton billboards of free expression were not allowed in the Soviet days. T-shirts were subversive, along with that capitalist expression known as "blue jeans."

In Congo, I attended worship services where colored T-shirts became uniforms. Each choir had the same color—red or green. The ushers wore yellow tees. All the T-shirts were castoffs that didn't sell in the U.S. or Europe. They were shipped to Africa and Asia in huge cargo containers. I'd seen stores made up of open containers and piles of T-shirts with customers picking through to find what they wanted. There in church I often read obscene messages on the shirts, but these worshippers didn't know the meaning of the English crudeness. Instead their T-shirt was chosen for its color so they could look like a unit with their brothers and sisters serving God together.

I have my grey and red Nebraska T-shirt given to me by the guys at a Baptist men's retreat in that state. I was new to the national staff doing peace work when their speaker cancelled at the last moment. I was the only national staff person available. I'd heard stories about how narrow-minded the folks in western Nebraska were, and I was doing peace work during the days of the Cold War and the wars in Central America. They desperately wanted me to come in spite of my repeated assertions that I'd have to talk about peace. We had a great time together, breaking each other's stereotypes and forming special bonds. So when I wear that Nebraska T-shirt, I'm not making a statement about the Cornhuskers. Rather, I'm reminding myself and anybody who will listen to the story about peace coming when we accept each other and learning from each other no matter how different we are.

I have so many T-shirts. Some I wear on the warm days. Some I use for painting and other messy work. Some I wear under my flannel shirts as the weather gets colder. I have my sports championship T-shirts to remember good days in Detroit—maybe someday I'll have a Lions championship shirt to go with my Tigers, Red Wings and Pistons collection! I have T-shirts from Zimbabwe, Italy, Ethiopia, Georgia,

Indonesia, Nagaland, Myanmar and Thailand. Each has a story. Each is woven with memories of people, places and peace work. If you don't believe it, I've got the T-shirt!

CHAPTER 4

We Are the Socks

HOW DID A chapter on T-shirts get into the Socks Saga? After telling the story of "You Are the Socks" at one event, I was surprised by the gift of a T-shirt. A woman had been moved by the story and made a special T-shirt for me. On the back of the olive-colored shirt was the sketch of a pair of socks and the simple word above them: SOCKS. In addition to the T-shirt, she gave me a large plastic bag full of socks she had collected by retelling the story.

When Sharon and I went to Kenya to lead a 10-day Training of Conflict Transformation Trainers, I realized what I could do with my bags of socks. I packed them all in a suitcase. During the training I shared the socks story in all its

Philip Kakungulu (in hat) at the 10-day training in Kenya.

chapters. At the end I challenged all the participants that they were the socks. God was calling them to cover some of the places of pain, brokenness and trauma in the world. I invited each of them to take a pair of socks as a reminder of who they were and their call to make a difference in the world.

One of those participants was Philip Kakungulu from Uganda, who also goes by the name Philip Stargate. Philip is a Christian teacher, youth leader, radio personality and activist. He took the socks story literally. He called the pair of socks he got his

Phillip wears his peace socks for a human rights run.

"peacemaker socks." Upon returning home, every time Philip would conduct a peacemaking workshop he would wear his peacemaker socks. He posted a picture of them on Facebook.

Philip Kakungulu leads a peace-building workshop in Uganda, demonstrating "turn the other cheek."

Philip is also a runner. He ran in a human rights race calling for respect of basic human rights for people in the gay and lesbian community. In Uganda, homosexuals have been treated with utmost contempt and violence. Philip joined in the call for gays and lesbians to have their basic human rights protected, running in his peacemaker socks.

Philip's peacemaker socks have traveled throughout Uganda as he works for justice and peace. He traveled to northern Kenya to work with Boaz Keibarak in facilitating conflict transformation workshops with the Pokot and Turkana people. He wore his socks on a peace walk between Pokot and Turkana villages that had been engaged in deadly warfare. He is planning to travel with his socks to South Sudan on a peacemaking mission.

We don't have to literally wear special socks to work or walk for peace. Philip does, but his heart is the real key as a peacemaker. The challenge is to hear the call to engage in the brokenness of the world and to be part of the solution rather than the problem. If we do that in whatever way we can wherever we can, we are the socks for justice and peace. We are the socks meant to cover the pain of the world. If we are the socks, others will be able to join us in that journey. They will walk—and run—to make a better future for us all.

PART 2

Kenya Chronicles

Beginning in 2011, I made a number of peacemaking trips to Kenya, working mostly with a Kenyan Christian activist named Wilson Gathungu. Wilson and I went to many places together, sometimes with my wife and others as part of our team. We had some adventures along the way. Here are some of the stories from our peace travels in that beautiful land.

CHAPTER 5

Building and Planting Peace—Literally

SHARON JUMPED INTO the mud with her bare feet and rolled up pants. She was joined by an older couple. They held hands and danced in the mud as fresh water was poured in and the red soil mashed to make more and more mud. Then, with our bare hands we scooped out the mud and put big gobs of it between the green sticks nailed on supporting timbers to make the wall.

A new house was being built for a family that had been displaced by the horrific violence that followed Kenya's national election in late 2007 and into 2008 that left some 1,500 people dead, hundreds of thousands of people displaced, and countless homes and businesses destroyed. Thousands of families were still living in Internally Displaced People (IDP) camps with tiny shelters of nylon and plastic sheeting. Now a family would have a new home.

Sharon and I were part of a peace-training team in 2011 led by Wilson Gathungu and the Rosell family from Central

Baptist Theological Seminary where Wilson was a student. Wilson had left Kenya for the U.S., eventually getting a college degree and entering seminary. In a Christian ethics course led by Terry Rosell, Wilson wrote a paper about the political violence in Kenya. Professor Rosell challenged Wilson to turn the paper into a project.

Author helping put up a roof for a family displaced by the post-election violence in Kenya.

So Wilson left Kansas City to return to his homeland. Thus was born the Kenya Peace Initiative—the project Wilson developed to build peace in the Molo District, one of the most volatile flashpoints for the cycles of electoral violence. The two major ethnic groups facing off in Molo were the Kikuyus and the Kalenjins, though other tribes were also involved in the violence.

Before leaving, Wilson, Terry and I consulted about what might be done. After Wilson organized an inter-ethnic planning team, Sharon, the Rosell family and I journeyed to Kenya to launch the initiative. The core of the trip was a five-day training and reconciliation program, which began with a day of reconciliation projects in the larger community.

We traveled to the Lancuenda IDP camp where people had been living for over three years. Camps like Lancuenda were scattered all around the countryside—camp "villages" much like the villages these people once lived in. They had tents from the U.N. and USAID. A small police outpost was just outside the camp to protect the inhabitants from further violence.

The IDP community welcomed us into their homes, such as they were. We heard their stories of trauma and loss. Then we helped to build two houses that were paid for out of the training program budget. The basic timbers had been raised already. So we helped put up the roof joists, a task at which I excelled with my height. Then we nailed up the long sticks that made the structure of the walls.

That's when Sharon jumped in to make the mud. We later learned that her action was a shock to the building participants because mud-making was a lower status task. Sharon's willing and playful spirit was noted as a model of the spirit necessary for reconciliation work. What made this a reconciliation project was that our group included Kikuyus and Kalenjins working together side-by-side. As one unified team, we built a home for a Kalenjin family and a home for a Kikuyu family. "The enemy" was rebuilding homes destroyed in the election crisis.

Sharon Buttry mixing mud with the couple who house was being built.

After washing off our feet and hands we traveled to the village of Kuresoi, a hotspot in the Molo District violence. We went to a school where hundreds of people joined with us to plant a "peace forest." We all carried seedlings to the corner of the school grounds at an intersection of the two main roads in town where a number of people had been slaughtered. Holes had been prepared for each seedling. Each tree had a student's name attached to it—students from the three main ethnic groups of that area who had been in conflict: Kikuyus, Kalenjins and Kisiis. I planted a tree along with a girl who was assigned to care for it. All across the field little knots of adults and students patted the soil with their bare hands.

A handmade peace pole was planted amid the forest with this prayer in all the local languages: "May peace prevail on earth." A commemorative plaque was unveiled. We had a big rally with dignitaries making speeches about peace and reconciliation. The culmination was a feast where we all "ate out of one pot," enjoying the specialties of each ethnic group.

Throughout the day I had amazing conversations with displaced people, journalists and church leaders. I heard their stories of struggle as well as their concerns and hopes. The day's activities were a practicum for opening our peace training. We were literally doing peace-building and literally planting the seeds of peace. You can't just talk peace and reconciliation, you have to do it!

CHAPTER 6

Raining on Our Parade

THE RAINS POURED and poured, soaking the hundreds of people marching for peace through the streets of Molo in Kenya. The deluge started just as we turned down a side street into the Molo town stadium, where we were scheduled to have a peace rally. By the time we got to the shelter at the stadium, which wasn't big enough to cover everyone, we were all soaked to the skin and shivering with cold. We set up a wall of umbrellas to protect us from the driving rain, which turned to hail a couple of times. Everything for our rally was wet. The soccer field had turned into puddles and mud. In the U.S., the event would have been cancelled, and people would have gone home disappointed. But this was Africa, and the rainy season is part of the rhythm of life.

This was the closing event for the five-day reconciliation and training program Wilson Gathungu had organized for the Molo District. We started with the reconciliation projects in the previous chapter. Then we had three days of intensive conflict transformation training. This culminated into our Sunday peace rally or convention in Molo town, the district center.

❧

The Salvation Army band gets ready to lead the peace parade.

When all the participants from the training returned to their home villages, Wilson sent them back with rented *matatus*, the minivans that are the backbone of the Kenyan transportation system. Following church services in their villages, people gathered back in Molo that afternoon. We had Baptists, Pentecostals, Catholics, Anglicans, Presbyterians and Salvation Army "soldiers"—a gathering of religious diversity.

We gathered at a key intersection in downtown Molo with hundreds of people lining the streets. The 60 or so training participants all stood out in the crowd wearing our white "Kenya Peace Initiative" baseball hats. The Salvation Army band led the way, and motorcycles made noise with their engines and horns to get attention. The lead marchers stretched out the Kenya Peace Initiative banner. As we marched through the streets of Molo, many onlookers joined us to make their witness for peace.

Just as we turned down the side street to the stadium it started to rain—not cats and dogs, but rhinos and elephants! The deluge went on and on and on. Many of us popped up umbrellas, but the ground quickly turned to mire and our lower halves were completely drenched. Those without umbrellas or coats were soaked clear through, including the band members.

There was a simple, open wood structure with a tin roof along the side of the walled field, but the roof was so high that the wind blew the rain into that area as well. We huddled under the shelter and formed a wall of umbrellas to provide some protection. I wondered what we would do. Was there an alternative plan? Should we just call it a day and go back to our places to dry off and warm up?

But, again, this was Africa. There is a determination and resiliency you don't find where life is easier.

Folks were rejoicing in the rain, because rain brings life. There had been a drought, and many were worried that some people might go hungry. So we praised God as the rains pelted us. The band quickly regrouped and began to play vigorously. Old women moved to the front and danced. Pastor Grace, one of our training participants, was in her dress with the Kenyan flag's colors. She waved a palm branch and eventually led the band and a few intrepid folks out in a procession around the field in the rain and mud. Grace was like Joshua leading people around Jericho—only in this instance she was claiming this place for God in the name of the Prince of Peace.

After almost an hour the rain finally slowed and eventually halted. The sun even came out briefly. People set up to start the rally even if we were delayed and all soaking wet.

First, there was lots of music. We moved out from the shelter and into the muddy field. Chairs were dried off and people got on

Continuing the parade in the rain and mud.

the stage. After lots of vigorous singing, the youth gave presentations and poems on peace themes. One young person's poem was incredibly direct at people in power and called for the giving up of weapons. Wilson spoke about the peace initiative. I preached on Romans 12:21, "*Overcome evil with good.*" Pastor Simon, who had translated much of the workshop, was my translator for the sermon. He and I were like a choreographed team preaching side-by-side.

Author speaks to the crowd at the peace rally in Molo.

Terry Rosell then called the children to the front of the stage. Some were smiling and laughing, but many wore deep serious faces of children who have seen too much suffering already in their young lives. Terry said our peacemaking was for them. He called us all to say "never again" to the children in English, Swahili and all the tribal tongues. Voices were raised in waves of language on the Pentecost Sunday saying "never again," and "peace forever, *Imani Milele*"!

Though it rained on our parade, the spirit of the event was even richer and more determined. Peace will require such determination if it is to be brought forth, whether in Kenya or in our own places of conflict. Storms come, but dedicated peacemakers need to keep the vision, be determined and press ahead.

CHAPTER 7

"We Are for Peace, But ..."

THE OLD POKOT man stood up to speak in response to our peace presentations. The villagers were gathered around with men sitting in a semicircle under one huge shade tree and women and young children clustered on the other side with their thatched huts behind them. Behind us about 50 yards was the river where earlier in the week a woman had been shot and killed by people from the Turkana village on the other side. She had simply been going down to the river to get water.

The village elder stood up slowly. "We want peace," he began, "but ... " He then spoke about this virus as if a bug was biting and infecting him, reaching down and pinching the back of his thigh. With a dramatic flair he flung out his arm pointing across the river. "Those people are the bugs! They are the virus! We want peace, but they don't. So we have to squash them!" He ground his foot into the dust.

"We want peace, but ... " As usual what is truly important is what is said after the "but ... "

∽

Wilson Gathungu and I had been invited to West Pokot, a large region in northwest Kenya, by Pini Kidulah. She was a Kenyan woman who had been in one of my 10-day training programs in the U.S. while she was in grad school. When she heard I was coming to Kenya, she invited me to Kapenguria to do some conflict transformation training. The region was plagued by chronic violence revolving around a culture of cattle rustling and intertribal conflict.

We finished the three-day workshop in Kapenguria. One of the participants was a pastor from the Pokot village in Turkwel (in the eastern end of West Pokot County) and invited us to come and speak to his villagers. Turkwel was about a two-hour drive from Kapenguria. But it wasn't the distance that gave us pause. It was the threat of violence. Recently, vehicles had been shot at in the region and the police were afraid to go there. Should we risk it? After discussion, we ascertained that all vehicles that had been shot at were government cars. We had been planning to borrow a government car but decided that wasn't a wise course of action! Instead, we hired a private taxi and headed to Turkwel.

Turkwel village.

Our team consisted of Pini, Wilson, Boaz Keibarak and me. Boaz was only in his early 20s but had already been chosen as a District Peace Commissioner. It was a nice-sounding government position, but he had little budgetary support. With great passion and commitment, however, Boaz plunged into mediation between conflicted groups in the region. Boaz had been an organizer, along with Pini, of the training we had done in Kapenguria and participated in the workshop. He told us about his regular trips to Turkwel, going back and forth between the Pokot and Turkana villages trying to help them end their spirals of violence. This young man went unarmed into a region where the police feared to go. Now, we were going with him.

We drove for a couple of hours along a highway that snaked through the mountains. Then, the road turned off into a scrubland national park. At some landmark we cut off into the bush with no road or path to guide us. After a few miles, we came to the village.

The men were already gathered in a semicircle under the tree. After we were seated, a parade of school children marched up singing songs of welcome. Pini, Wilson and I all made presentations about the ways to peace. We were politely received. Then the elder stood up: "We want peace, but … "

Boaz (in white shirt) speaks at Turkwel village gathering.

I'd heard that same sentiment voiced in my own country, even in churches where I challenge people to follow the teaching of Jesus, to do the things that make for peace. "Yes, we all want peace, but … " We bring a "realism" that counters and discounts the "idealism" of Jesus, even though we claim to follow Jesus. People of any faith who speak about peace may be nice and present lovely thoughts, but we have to be realistic, don't we? Jesus calls us to love our enemies, but "those people over there" are not peace-loving like us. They are a deadly virus that we must rid of before we can have peace. We want peace, but … those people always get in the way.

Wilson and I looked at each other. This encounter wasn't going so well. But young Boaz stood up and gently and graciously, yet firmly challenged the elder's view. Peace can be possible, but someone has to risk taking the steps of reconciliation toward the other side. Boaz, a Pokot himself, had repeatedly taken the risk to go across the river and talk to the Turkana people. He was opening up the communication by going back and forth. He challenged the realism of resignation to violence voiced by the elder with a realism of hope that knows how to roll up its sleeves and get to work.

The women and children of Turkwel listened patiently to our presentations.

We didn't make peace that day, but we did bring a connection of support and encouragement to a village on the edge of survival and violence. Boaz showed us the courage and ongoing commitment that it takes to challenge the "but … " that undermines hopes for peace. We stood with him, giving the support for which he asked. It was clear to me, though, that we weren't the main peacemakers here. The main peacemaker was Boaz—a young man who dared, who risked, who wasn't intimidated by the "but … "

What is our "but … " that we bring to the possibilities of peace? What is the "realistic" correction we bring that blocks us from new possibilities? Our settings and situations may be very different, but the conversation is a familiar one. May we find the courage to press on through the "but … " within us and around us and create the future that is more possible than we think.

CHAPTER 8

The Dividing Highway

ROADS OFTEN BRING people together. They are the connectors that allow people to get from place to place, to trade goods and services, to come from their various dwelling places to gather for special events. But not in Mauche, a village beyond the town of Nukuru in Kenya. The road from Nukuru to Mauche became a dividing line, separating the Kikuyus from the Kalenjins. That road was as effective a barrier as the Berlin Wall for an earlier generation or the Great Wall of China centuries ago. The "Great Wall of Mauche" was a simple tarmac road.

During the December 2007 election and spilling over into 2008, political violence in Kenya cut down tribal lines, leaving over a thousand people dead. Mauche and the surrounding villages were hot spots in the conflict. Kikuyus and Kalenjins, in particular, slaughtered each other. After the worst violence ceased, the Kikuyus and Kalenjins remained deeply divided. Mauche was one village, but its people were on opposite sides of the highway separated along tribal lines. Though everyone lived in the same village, they did not dare to cross the street. Everyone could remember the terrible acts of violence and destruction done by those people on the other side of the road.

When I was in Mauche in 2012, the divisions were still very deep. A new election was coming up, and people were extremely anxious. Would there be more violence, more bloodletting, more deaths, more homes destroyed, more people seeking shelter in the IDP camps that still dotted the hillsides?

I came to Mauche with Wilson Gathungu, director of the Peacemaking, Reconciliation And Rehabilitation Initiative (PRARI). In 2011 Wilson had brought a team of us to lead a training and series of reconciliation actions in the Molo District, which includes Mauche. So now Wilson and I had come to Mauche to do a follow-up training conference and peace rally.

For three days, Wilson and I conducted a workshop in a small, corrugated metal church along the dividing highway. The Rev. Kones, the pastor of the church, had been in the Molo District training in 2011. Now he hosted a mixed group of over 50 Kalenjins, Kikuyus and Maasais. We studied the Bible about peace together. We ate together out of a common serving pot, a Kenyan sign of unity. We danced together and praised God together.

On Sunday, after worshiping in various churches, we gathered on the highway at the east end of town. All the workshop participants and various friends, family members and church members joined us. The Salvation Army band led the way as we processed through town down the dividing highway to witness to our oneness in the determination and build a positive future. Motorcycle taxis added to the celebrative din. As we walked together down this road, we waved for people watching from both sides to join us. Many stepped out and became part of the parade.

In a schoolyard at the center of town we held our rally. Wilson and I preached about peace. Various choirs from Mauche churches sang about peace. A workshop participant recited poetry he had written about peace. Men, women and children, many in traditional garb, enthusiastically danced for peace. At the end of the rally, three doves were released by Kalenjin, Kikuyu and Maasai participants.

There are so many lines of division among us. Some are borders protected by huge walls such as the "Security Barrier" between Israel and Palestine. Some are low, physical barriers with high social stigmas that mark off "the other side of the tracks." Some barriers are marked by cloth-

Author on the Dividing Highway.

ing styles or colors so our identity is quickly evident: We are of this tribe, not that one. Our divisions can be lighthearted such as over school rivalries, or they can be fraught with the weight of the divine over religious differences. Our identities are vital and important, but must they split us apart? How do we cross the dividing highways to create stronger communities?

At the west end of Mauche, as people spread out into the surrounding rural areas and farms, the memories of the violence were still painfully present. But in one small rural area people overcame the division. They too had a dividing road, in this case a dirt track that came down from the highway winding to a little vale with a stream flowing through it. Kikuyus lived on the north side of the dirt road, Kalenjins on the south.

The healing of this community began with those who had suffered the most in the fighting—in this case the Kalenjins. The Kalenjin elders decided to approach the elders of their enemies, the Kikuyus. They came with words of reconciliation and a specific proposal for a project to bind their shattered community together. Everyone needed decent water. The stream flowed between the Kalenjins and the Kikuyus, but animals fouled the stream as they came to drink. People from both sides were getting sick from the polluted water. It took a few

Wilson Gathungu leads a peacemaking workshop in Mauche.

months for trust to be built, but the Kalenjin elders persisted in expressing their good intentions and their vision for a solution to a common problem.

Their idea was to work together to build a small dam to make a reservoir that they would all share. The safe drink-

Walking for peace together down the Dividing Highway.

ing water now comes from the reservoir and the animals are watered downstream. Women do their washing together. The men work on tree nurseries together, reforesting their region. Kalenjins and Kikuyus are even picnicking together near the reservoir. So these folks eagerly came to join us for both the peace workshops and the march down the highway.

Division can be overcome. But it doesn't happen by chance or accident. People must take the risks to start the process. Sometimes, the risk-taking courage comes from those who have been hurt the most—the victims. Sometimes, someone has to step away from their secure sanctuary into the rough and tumble of common space. Someone has to be like the Kalenjin elders who approached the Kikuyu elders. Someone has to be like Wilson, who left the seminary classroom to go to the flash points of political and tribal violence. Someone bridges the division with their action and, eventually, the dividing highway becomes the artery for the lifeblood of a new community.

The peace parade down the Dividing Highway.

CHAPTER 9

Arriving on Broken Pieces

THE TEXT FOR the special graduation service cited Acts 27 about the shipwreck when the apostle Paul was being taken to Rome as a prisoner. As I heard the Scripture being read I wondered: What on earth! This is a terrible text for such a moment. How little I knew.

The preacher was Dr. Henry Mugabe from Zimbabwe. Dr. Mugabe is a great soul. He had taken over a struggling Baptist seminary in his homeland and in 16 years turned it into such a premier institution that the Anglican Church was sending some of their most promising seminarians to study there. He had academic rigor, but also an incredibly gracious spirit. Some of his actions—supporting women in ministry, having ecumenical ties and doing theology out of African cultural contexts—upset fundamentalist Baptists. The fundamentalists engaged in a takeover that forced Dr. Mugabe out. Later a new seminary was founded with many of the professors from the old one, so Henry Mugabe knows about shipwrecked dreams and visions.

We were in Kenya for a 10-day Training of Conflict Transformation Trainers (TCTT) that I'd developed to equip key peacemaking leaders and activists around the world. We had academic folks such as Dr. Mugabe. We had pastors and denominational leaders from conflict zones. We also had peace, human rights and environmental activists in their 20s and 30s. It was an amazing mix of people from eight African countries and the U.S.

The local coordinator was Wilson Gathungu, and he was the one graduating. Wilson was a student from Central Baptist Theological Seminary (CBTS) in Kansas City. While taking a Christian ethics course, he wrote a paper about the post-election violence in his homeland of Kenya and what the church should do about it. Wilson's professor said what Wilson did should be a project, not just a paper.

So Wilson left the U.S., where he had lived for many years, and went back to Kenya. He developed an extensive reconciliation initiative in the Molo District of the Rift Valley, known as one of the flash points in the cycles of political violence that had rocked Kenya. From 2011 through 2013, I worked with Wilson on some of the training programs and

Dr. Henry Mugabe preaching about getting home on broken pieces.

peace rallies that he organized. I would bring new textbooks from Central Seminary so Wilson could finish his remaining courses for his master's degree by completing his work online and using email to communicate with the professors.

When Wilson finished his studies, he was invited to travel back to Kansas City for graduation with his class. However, the U.S. wouldn't give him a visa. The visa he had acquired earlier expired when he returned to Kenya to carry out the peace work. In spite of many people appealing on his behalf, Wilson was denied the opportunity to participate in the graduation.

So Central sent the graduation to Wilson. Three Central students traveled to Kenya for the TCTT, carrying with them a letter from CBTS's president, Dr. Molly Marshall. I had been given an honorary doctorate from CBTS, so I could represent the school as well. Dr. Mar-

Wilson speaks at his graduation.

shall sent me Wilson's framed diploma, and we added in a cap and gown. We took a break from the training and prepared for Wilson's graduation ceremony.

After various opening remarks and greetings, Dr. Mugabe began to preach and launched from the text about the apostle Paul being shipwrecked. The text in Acts 27 speaks of those who could jump into the water and swim; others held on to the pieces and planking of the ship as it broke up on the reef. In spite of the danger of the storm and the shipwreck, everyone made it safely to shore.

Dr. Mugabe talked about coming "home," landing safely on the shore "on broken pieces." He knew about the broken pieces of church conflict that shattered his seminary. He knew about character assassination from people who should be supporters. He was speaking to a graduate who knew about the politics of privilege that denied a poor black African the opportunity to graduate with his classmates to receive an honor he had earned. So many of us there knew of broken pieces. We had participants who lived with daily violence in war zones; people who knew the fear of hiding from insurgents seeking children to kidnap and turn into young soldiers; people who had seen churches bombed; and young folks who knew their economic futures were severely restricted. We all had hopes, but we were swimming amid the broken pieces of conflict, injustice and fear. Yet, here we were celebrating Wilson's graduation, maybe not where and how it had once been dreamed but in a profound and special way nonetheless. By God's grace we do find the way home. We do get safely to the shore, even sometimes clinging to the broken pieces. Dr. Mugabe's message gave all gathered that day an image that we have recalled many times to each other in our times of struggle—we will get home, perhaps even on broken pieces.

PART 3

Trails of Tears

Peacemaking puts you into many conflicted situations, and with violence comes trauma. There are many sad stories and tragic tales you hear—and sometimes enter into intimately. Along the trail of tears, however, hope often springs up in surprising ways. I look for ways the tears are transformed. Sometimes, the tears themselves become the catalysts for transformation.

CHAPTER 10

Drying the Tears of Jesus

I WAS HOTTER than I'd ever been standing on a tarmac under the sweltering sun in Congo. We had just flown into Kikwit from Kinshasa. Our luggage had been dumped in a pile on the tarmac, and we had to wait standing in the sun while officials checked through our documents. We waited about 45 minutes.

As we stood there, I could hear singing drifting from the other side of the airport fence. The only word I could make out was "*mbote*," repeated over and over. "What does *mbote* mean?" I asked Virgil Nelson, my missionary colleague and traveling companion. He told me that *mbote* is the greeting in the Kikongo language. It's a term like "shalom" in Hebrew or "aloha" in Hawaiian, a very rich term wishing the fullness of blessing and goodness upon the one being greeted.

I could barely make out the choir singing *mbote* in the distance. They were a shimmer of color—black, yellow and gold. I told Virgil, "Looks like some VIP flew in with us." But as I gazed around, I didn't see anybody who looked like a VIP, just a lot of sweaty impatient passengers wanting to get out of the sun as soon as possible.

I was on the flight into Kikwit because the Rev. Ikomba, General Secretary of the Community of Baptists in Western Congo (CBCO) and Virgil invited me to Congo to lead conflict transformation workshops. Congo had been going through the worst war on the planet since

Author being greeted by the choir at Kikwit airport.

World War II. We were leading a series of workshops, including a three-day program in Kikwit.

Finally, our documents were stamped and returned to us. As the three of us passed through the gate of the airport, a little girl ran up to Rev. Ikomba and gave him a bouquet of flowers. Then we were all ushered into a receiving line to be greeted by 20 pastors from the area and by the 60 members of the choir who were still vigorously singing *mbote. We* were the VIPs!

We were led to a car to begin a slow caravan toward the church, where the training would be held. Behind us, the choir members piled into pickup trucks, continuing their singing. When we got to the church, more people were eagerly awaiting

Teaching the things that make for peace in Congo.

us. The church's school let the children out for the celebration. The crowd picked up the choir's singing of *mbote*. Children mobbed the car. I had to swim my way through the kids, reaching out and touching as many hands as I could while pushing my way into the church.

Inside, the sanctuary was packed. We were treated to a welcome service, complete with more music from the choir. I had never been greeted like this in all my travels.

Children greeting guests as they arrive in Kikwit.

Then I learned I was supposed to preach. Nobody had warned me about this, so I had nothing prepared. I was wearing blue jeans for the travel day, but that didn't matter, as most people were dressed poorly and simply. What mattered was the joy about us coming.

So in the moments I had during the service to gather my thoughts, all I could think of was another joyous welcome: the moment when Jesus entered into Jerusalem on what we now call Palm Sunday. There was singing that day as well. Children ran around joyously, stripping branches off the palms and waving them exuberantly. The shouts of "Hosanna!" echoed like *mbote* from the stone walls of Jerusalem.

But amid all the celebration, Jesus wept. When he came over the brow of the hill called the Mount of Olives, he saw the city spread out before him and began to cry. As he wept he said, *"Oh, that today you knew the things that make for peace! But now they are hidden from your eyes"* (Luke 19:42). I was delighted to be greeted in such an effusive way, but the greeting was poignant.

Why was I in Kikwit? Because of conflict! Obviously there was the war going on, which was to leave over 4 million people dead. Even while we were doing the workshop, we were interrupted one afternoon by the rhythmic stamping of about 50 or 60 young men being quick-marched past the church on their way to being inducted into the Congolese army. War was our ever-present context. But I was also there because of the war within the Baptist churches. Ethnic clashes were hindering the unity and the effectiveness of their collective witness during a time of national crisis. Conflict within the church was preventing conflict transformation work outside the church. I envisioned Jesus weeping even amid the warm and sweet reception going on.

"Oh, that today you knew the things that make for peace, but they are hidden from your eyes." Congo wasn't the only place at war. My own country was at war as well, a war against terrorism that has had many battlefields and fronts and little constructive resolution. The things that make for peace seemed hidden from Congolese and American eyes, surely something over which to weep!

Author speaking at the spot where Jesus wept over Jerusalem.

But as I was there with these celebrating sisters and brothers in Kikwit, aware of the sorrow of the fighting going on, I was also keenly aware of the purpose of our coming together. I had been brought in specifically to teach the things that make for peace. There was a hunger to learn the skills of conflict transformation and to put them into practice.

That's why I was there. That's why people were so excited about my coming. That's why pastors can come from churches all around in that district, bringing their key leaders with them.

As I sat there, I was given a vision of Jesus weeping and us drying his tears. We were seeking to learn those things that make for peace. We were planning to put those things into practice in families, congregations, communities and in the larger society where possible. So if we were learning and doing the things that make for peace, were we not also drying the tears of Jesus?

That image has stayed with me from that moment in Kikwit. There are many things that make Jesus weep, many actions of violence and injustice that destroy life in one way or another. Each of the actions we take to affirm life, to undo oppression, to establish justice, to forge peace, to heal wounds brings joy to the grieving heart of Jesus. We wipe away his tears through our acts that reflect his heart.

I had an opportunity to visit the traditional spot of the Mount of Olives where Jesus wept over the city of Jerusalem. I was with a group of American Jews and Protestant Christians engaged in dialog for understanding, justice and peace. We were exploring concerns from both the Israeli and Palestinian sides of the contemporary conflict. I was invited to share this vision of Jesus weeping at that site and to speak about our efforts to dry those tears.

Jesus continues to weep over our various cities and countries. Where do you see him weeping? Are you doing those things that make for peace that might be drying his tears? I can think of no better work to do.

CHAPTER 11

A Tale of Two Memorials

CHARLES DICKENS' CLASSIC, *A Tale of Two Cities,* begins with the immortal lines, "It was the best of times, it was the worst of times." His story unfolds amid the turmoil of revolutionary France in a time that brought out the best and worst in people.

When I traveled in the nations born out of the shattering war that dismembered Yugoslavia, I saw similar contrasts. In Croatia and Bosnia I saw memorials about the war. There was the memorial on the bridge in Sarajevo to mark the deaths of two young people shot down by snipers. They were the first to die in what became a long, horrific siege. There was the memorial in Tuzla to scores of people killed when a mortar shell landed among a fun-loving crowd one evening during a ceasefire. The names of Croats, Bosnians and Serbs were inscribed together on the wall because they were killed together. However, they weren't buried together. Each ethnic group was divided along religious lines and buried in their respective cemeteries: Croats in the Catholic cemetery, Serbs in the Orthodox cemetery and Bosnians in the Muslim cemetery.

A small memorial for journalists killed in the war was chiseled into a stone plaque on a street corner in Sarajevo. It named a casualty of all such times of spiraling violence: Truth. Some journalists are killed just because of the risks of covering armed conflict, but some are deliberately targeted, for the work they do is the enemy.

The contrast was greatest at two places where the most extreme brutalities of the war were made evident. The names speak of what the wars in former Yugoslavia came to epitomize: Vukovar and Srebrenica.

∾

I visited Vukovar 12 years after the war between Serbia and Croatia. The fighting around Vukovar became the occasion to introduce a new phrase into the English language: ethnic cleansing. The Serb army tried to drive Croats out of the land they held by stimulating the fear of slaughter for any Croat who dared to stay.

Vukovar was still a devastated city when I visited. There were mounds of rubble where houses once stood. A massive factory that once employed 20,000 workers was a large complex of shattered walls, metal and concrete skeletons, weeds and wind. Large apartment complexes were ghost towns of blasted brick. The only buildings that were not more than half destroyed were the

Memorial at the pig farm outside Vukovar.

new structures put up since the war. Some of the streets had new houses. The downtown area had hulking shells next to a new glass structure. War makes the news, but rebuilding goes on without much attention. One former soldier I spoke to said, "This is my city; I'm not leaving."

The ruins were stark reminders of what happened and the ferocity of ethnic hatred. Their witness, however, was mute.

A memorial outside of town told the story. The most notorious incident in the fight for Vukovar was what happened at the hospital. The Serb militia captured the hospital. All the doctors, nurses, staff and patients were taken to a pig farm where they were butchered and buried under the pig slop. The

The memorial for Croats from the Vukovar hospital who were murdered.

memorial was raised by Croats after the Serbs were driven back. A huge black monolith rises out of a field with the silhouette of a dove carved near the top for the sky to shine through. From a distance it looks beautiful, but up close the words are chilling. Inscribed into marble at the base are words that speak of "the murderous Serbs" who did this—implying that all Serbs are guilty, not just the Serb militiamen who perpetrated the crime.

This hate is rooted in earlier cycles of violence. During World War II, the Croat fascists allied with Hitler's German Nazis. Serbs were the victims of fascist ethnic violence like the Jews, though not to as thorough a degree. Serbs were interned in concentration camps. The ethnic cleansing campaign of the 1990s was rooted in memories from the 1940s. The more recent violence had fueled fresh hatred with the ghosts of

Croatian Nazis being revived in neo-Nazis today. I taught at a seminary in Osijek, about 18 kilometers (about 11 miles) from Vukovar. Outside the seminary gate is a Serbian Orthodox church. Painted on the church gate was a swastika. The memorial at the pig farm serves not to heal but to stir up new hatred.

Three years later, I was back in the region, and my hosts took me to visit the Bosnian town of Srebrenica. Srebrenica was the scene of the worst massacre in Europe since the end of World War II. On July 11, 1995, over 8,000 Muslim men and boys of all ages were slaughtered by Serbian militiamen. The women were driven out while fathers, husbands, brothers and sons were buried in mass graves.

When I visited, Srebrenica was like a ghost town, having experienced little of the rebuilding seen in other parts of Bosnia. It stands as a testament to the "success" of ethnic cleansing—for the Muslim survivors of the town live elsewhere.

A large memorial complex has been established. Ironically, it is guarded on the outside by Serb police from the Republic of Srpska, the scattered political entity that marks where Bosnian Serbs live. The killers still live in the town and

A Qur'anic quote about the possibility of enemies becoming friends at the Srebrenica Memorial.

perhaps are even among the police guarding the memorial to the people they killed.

Inside the memorial grounds, I found both horror and hope. As I came in, I was confronted with a huge circle of low, sloped, massive blocks of granite. Into the granite were carved the 8,000 names and ages of the men and boys massacred that day. Eight thousand is such an abstract figure until you try to read name upon name upon name. I saw the names of a 2-year-old child and a 76-year-old man.

I was visiting on the 11th day of March and stumbled onto the Mothers of Srebrenica holding their vigil. On the 11th of every month, they gather to commemorate the loss of their loved ones. So I walked and meditated among the grieving, praying mothers while some of the killers stood sentry outside.

The granite arc at the Srebrenic Memorial of the name of the massacred men and boys.

The week before I arrived in Bosnia, the International Court of Justice ruled that Serbia did not commit genocide related to the massacre in Srebrenica, merely that they failed to stop the Bosnian Serbs who did the killing. Larger political issues were at stake in efforts to bring Serbia into peace processes elsewhere in the region. So, the tortured logic of the court acknowledged that crimes had taken place but nobody could be held responsible.

With no justice for the killers and from the international community, what kind of memorial was raised by these grieving mothers? I was stunned by their witness.

Also in granite, near the circle of names, was a quote from the Quran. The quote was remarkable given the current context in Bosnia: *"It may be that God will bring about friendship*

between you and those whom you hold to be your enemies."
What a verse to choose! It spoke of hope for reconciliation that would ultimately break the cycles of hatred and violence, a hope that was prophetic and visionary with little support than from the faith of the women.

Further on, there was a cemetery. As the mass graves were unearthed, the remains that could be identified were put into fresh graves, each with a marker. Overlooking the new graves was a tall slab of stone with a prayer chiseled into it. The prayer, identified to be from the Mothers of Srebrenica, read: "In the name of God the Most Merciful and Most Compassionate, we pray to Almighty God, may grievance become hope, may revenge become justice, and may mothers' tears become prayers that Srebrenica never happen again to no one nowhere." To no one nowhere—not just to our people, but to all people. The Mothers gave an extraordinary expression of compassion for all people in a context where ethnocentrism was fought over most savagely and was still dramatically unresolved.

In these days, when our news is filled with fears of Muslims and terror done in the name of Islam, I remember Srebrenica. It was people who claimed to be Christians—Catholics and Orthodox—who slaughtered because of ethnic and religious differences. It was Muslim women who had been victims of that violence who presented a compassionate and hopeful alternative to the hate. Jesus commanded, *"Love your enemies."* Those who claimed to be followers of Jesus even slaughtered the defenseless. Grieving Muslim women who had yet to receive any justice were the ones who exhibited hearts more in line with Jesus.

How do we respond in the times of crisis? Do we find the worst coming out? Do we get swept up in fear, suspicion and hatred? Do we condone violence because of who "they" are? Or do we rise to the best when times are worst? Do we speak and act with compassion that brings the only hope for a better future?

CHAPTER 12

"Now I Understand the Serbs!"

NOW I UNDERSTAND the Serbs!" So said a traumatized Bosnian Muslim soldier, a veteran of the brutal war that raged in Bosnia. He was attending a workshop about trauma healing, and suddenly he gained a humanizing insight into the "enemy" that had treated him and his people so badly. How do we heal from deep horrific violence and find the way to reconciliation? That was the question before us in the aftermath of the Bosnian war.

On my first trip to Bosnia, I spent some time in Tuzla, one of the more ethnically mixed communities both during the war and afterward. I worked with Fyodor Raychynets, a Ukrainian Baptist missionary who was pastor of a small church in Tuzla. Fyodor invited me to do conflict transformation and trauma healing work in Bosnia.

The group we worked with was small—only 11 people—but they were a unique gathering for a Bible study. Six of the participants were Baptist or Pentecostal Christians, including some Serbian mothers. The other five were Muslim men from a support group for Bosnian army veterans with post-traumatic stress. Fyodor met one of the veterans and invited his support group to join us for the sessions.

We centered on the awful Bible story of Rizpah found in 2 Samuel 21. The Muslim vets were quite willing to plunge into the story, since it was not an issue of religious belief but of human experience. We had two evenings for the workshop. I planned to focus on Rizpah on the second night. Rizpah was

Fyodor Raychynets and author leading a workshop on trauma healing in Bosnia.

a mother whose two sons were executed under the orders of King David in a political killing with religious overtones. She's an amazing example of someone who moved through her trauma toward personal and community healing, but that's another part of the story.

On the first evening, we were going to look at two other responses to trauma in the story. One was the dynamics of victim/survivor were seen in Merab, another mother who lost all five of her sons under David's edict. Merab disappeared from the story, frozen forever as the victim.

The second was about the Gibeonites, an ethnic minority group in Israel. They suffered genocidal massacres under the reign of David's predecessor, King Saul. Through divine and political twists in the story, the Gibeonites seized the opportunity to turn their history of victimization into justification for new actions of violence. They were victims who then became victimizers—but you can't understand this switch without knowing the earlier story of their trauma and suffering and how it distorted and twisted them with shame, humiliation and hate.

As we worked through this ancient story, the participants recognized their own scenarios of horror and trauma they suffered. Like Merab, the permanent victim, they were still living with the powerful impact of those searing experiences with violence. The Muslim men were dealing directly in the PTSD support group with those traumas that had such a strong, haunting grip on them.

As we then considered the journey of the Gibeonites, the survivors of genocide who became killers, a healing revelation took place. A traumatized Muslim vet sitting right in front of me suddenly blurted out, "Now I understand the Serbs! They call me a Turk," he went on. "I'm not a Turk." With fresh eyes coming from this ancient story of the Gibeonites, he could understand the very people who had treated him so horribly he was still mentally scarred years later. "Turk" was an insulting term by Serbs for Muslims. It harkened back to the humiliating defeat of the Serbs centuries earlier by the Turkish army of the Ottoman Empire. Muslims, especially their Bosnian Muslim neighbors, were living reminders of that historic humiliation. Turk was an angry insult to hide the Serbs' own shame. With the disintegration of Yugoslavia, that humiliation and shame exploded in genocidal revenge.

Now I understand the Serbs. Part of healing is to recognize the humanity of the enemy. In our own traumatized pain, we want to demonize the enemy, to strip them of their humaness in some way. During the wars in former Yugoslavia, *Newsweek* magazine

Bosnian Muslim veterans share their trauma art.

ran a cover story about the Serbian ruler Slobodan Milošević. *Newsweek* put Milošević's photo on the cover with the title, "The Face of Evil." That's what we are all tempted to do when we are grievously hurt. We want to make out the other to be evil, which leaves us then as the "face of good." We're the good guys, so our enemy must be the bad guys.

Yet, stories are usually not so simple, not black and white, or perhaps black isn't evil and white isn't good. The ancient story in 2 Samuel 21 is complex, and the history in the Balkans is complex. Everyone is stained by the blood on the hands of their own people. Through the lens of this ancient story, the Muslim veteran could speak compassionately about the trauma at the root of the violence that marked his life. Out of trauma, empathy grew.

Bosnian Muslim veterans working on trauma healing through art.

At the end of the session, a Serbian Baptist woman asked the Muslim veterans if she could pray for them. Her own family had been shredded by the war, a pain she'd shared earlier in the session. The Serbian woman looked at me: "I'm not asking your permission, I'm asking theirs," turning toward the Bosnian Muslim men. The veterans agreed, and this Serbian woman, burdened with her own painful losses and memories, lifted up a beautiful prayer for the inner healing of the Muslim soldiers.

People who had once seen each other as enemies were coming with their wounds to understand, to pray and to form a healing community. It was a tiny community perhaps, but the power of that evening left Fyodor and me stunned with what we had witnessed. "This is one of the best nights in all the five years I've been in Bosnia," Fyodor said as we walked back to his apartment.

CHAPTER 13

The Pitted Porch

I HAD MY own story that helped me understand the Serbs. The story was embedded in the tiny pits dug into the concrete porch on the front of our house. At first I thought the pits were just a sign of a crumbling old house, then I learned that they held a story.

I lived in the city of Warren, Michigan when the war was going on between Serbia and Croatia, followed by the war between Serbia and Bosnia, followed by the war between Serbia and the Kosovar Albanians and then the bombing of Serbia by NATO. Our media was filled with the horrors of that war and the atrocities committed by Serbs who had coined the awful term "ethnic cleansing" to capture their strategic goal.

During that time of terrible war news from disintegrating Yugoslavia, my house told this story that made it impossible for me to demonize the Serbs being portrayed as such brutal monsters in our media. My neighbor filled me in on the story about the pits on the porch. The old, single man who owned

the house before us and died in it was a Serb. He survived
World War II.

∽

During World War II, Croat fascists known as the Ustaše
ruled under the German Nazis. They collaborated with Hitler
in the extermination of the Jews, but they also butchered over
300,000 Serbs. The man who lived in our house and one of his
aunts were the only survivors of an extended family of some
300 relatives. He lost almost everyone in his life.

This Serbian man survived the war because he had a skill
that was valuable in the concentration camp. He played the
cello. He was incorporated into the camp orchestra that
would play as the freight trains rolled into the death camp and
unloaded their human cargo. The music was supposed to calm
the terrified people so they could be murdered in an orderly
fashion.

The previous owner had gone through such horror and lost
his extended family simply because he was a Serb.

After the war, he came to the U.S. and settled in the Detroit
area. At some point he bought our house. He used to sit on the
front porch with his cello and dig out little divots for the cello
endpin. I imagine playing the cello on our porch was soothing
to his traumatized soul.

Our neighbor said that occasionally a long black limousine
would pull up to the house and an Asian man would get out.
My neighbor said it was Yo-Yo Ma, and that the Serb home-
owner had been his teacher long ago. I tried to contact Yo-Yo
Ma to verify the story but never got a response.

While the wars raged in the Balkans, though, and I
heard stories about the horrible Serbs, the pits on the porch
reminded me of the terrible things done to the Serbs. What
happened in the Holocaust didn't justify ethnic cleansing, but
knowing what had happened to the man who lived in our
house and the horrific losses he experienced let me know this

was recycled brutality and pain. I couldn't hate all Serbs. Serbian pain was etched into my own house.

I love Yo-Yo Ma's music because he uses it to bring people together, especially across cultural lines. Maybe, in the music of this old teacher, there was an alternative to dealing with the history of violence. Instead of letting the circle of hate go round and round and claim yet another generation of victims, maybe we can turn our pain into elegiac music. Maybe we can hear the emotions in our heart echoed back in the music of someone from the other side. Maybe we should sit on the porch together and play beautiful music through our tears.

CHAPTER 14

The Forgotten Calculation

"WHAT DO YOU do when your country is invaded?" That intense, passionately asked question came when I began to teach a course on conflict transformation at a seminary in Lebanon. We had students from all over the Middle East. The course had originally been scheduled a few months earlier, but we had to push the date back because the seminary became a refuge for people displaced during the war between Israel and Hizbullah. So this was not a theoretical question. It was a question with fresh memories of the Shiite Muslim families who had fled the bombed apartments of South Beirut for shelter up in a Baptist seminary in the Christian northern suburbs of the city.

I had been used to quieter students in many of the Asian contexts in which I'd been teaching. These Arab students were more vociferous, constantly asking blunt, high-energy questions. Besides the war that had exploded around them a few months earlier, many of these students came from highly conflicted and violent contexts in their home countries. They would wrestle with me as I challenged their concepts. We grappled with issues of nonviolence, loving enemies, reconciliation and transforming conflicts from the margins of society. Then, after a rip-roaring discussion, their faces would beam, and they would tell me they loved me.

∽

"What do you do when your country is invaded?" It was early in the course when one of the students asked this question. I had put him off saying that we needed to get into a number of topics first to lay the foundation for a good discussion of that question. So he waited until later in the course, and he posed it again. This time there was no ducking the question.

As we explored various dimensions of peacemaking—negotiation and mediation, nonviolence and community organizing—we came to the topic of trauma. We explored the costs in human lives and destroyed community in both violent and nonviolent struggles. So often people ignore the long-term impact of trauma that lasts for years after the bombs have stopped falling. The war in Lebanon had finished quickly, but I had seen the horrific damage of building after building in southern Beirut pancaked into concrete mountains. In people's eyes, though, I could see the deeper wounds; the internal scars that I knew would last far longer. I'd seen victims of similar conflicts decades after the violence that tore at their hearts and minds. We could hear the media leaders of Hizbullah crowing about how they had stood up to Israel, but the overwhelming cost of that brief war was all around me. I spoke about the weight of trauma as the forgotten calculation when wars are waged and "victories" celebrated. The emotional and psychological victims of violence are overlooked on all sides.

Then, one of the students spoke up. He had never shared in the class to that point. He was from a country that experienced a long, brutal war. I knew he was traumatized from the moment I first met him and saw his eyes. As we talked about trauma, he told his own story.

He had been show-
ing a film about Jesus
in his community. Sud-
denly, government
soldiers showed up and
surrounded the gath-
ering. He told about
being seized and put
inside a big gunny-
sack. Then the soldiers
beat him with rifle
butts. Those watching
him later compared his

**Destroyed apartment
building in southern Beirut.**

sufferings to what they had seen of Jesus in the movie. That sounds like a "good Christian testimony" of making some-thing spiritually good out of something terrible, but the student concluded saying, "I'm still traumatized."

Then, a second student spoke. He was much older, per-haps in his late 30s or early 40s. He had been a solider—an elite paratrooper in a major Middle Eastern army. He was a sergeant, someone who had risen to a level of leadership. That army used the Soviet model of training, which includ-ing beating soldiers to inure them to violence. He spoke of many recruits dying in basic training, including one of his close friends, "for no reason." Details of what he did as a sol-dier were just hinted at, but this student shared about his own emotional death with poignant specificity in order to function well as an elite soldier. As he got older, in desperation, he left the army to save his shriveling humanity. Now he was a semi-nary student, but he told us that he still feels numb most of the time. He was just beginning to recover from the brutalization he was a part of.

How do we hold the stories of others with such pain and trauma? We had just heard two very different stories from different ends of the gun. Our class time was almost over, but I felt we were in a holy moment. These two had risked so much to share their stories in this way. They had risked stripping off the mask of the myths we devise to hide the face of evil in violence. They showed what was in their own hearts at the cost of our war-making.

So we prayed. We came to the foot of the cross where Jesus transformed our human act of violence into the divine act of love, mercy, forgiveness and salvation. Jesus bore our sorrows, bore our sins and bore the sins committed against us. He bore it all.

Then, Jesus rises again, and he comes to us to touch us with healing. But the hands that touch are scarred. He is a wounded healer. His touch enables us to not only be healed, but to become wounded healers as well.

These students will always bear their scars, as we all will bear the scars in our experiences of brokenness. But God is at work to heal those deep wounds. Through their deep testimonies, these students were speaking truth as a step to heal the wounds of the world. They were telling us of the profound psychic cost of our choices for violence, both for the victims and users of violence. By speaking, these two students were already being used by God as healers—even in their pain.

Our natural tendency is to avoid the pain. In thinking about going to war, we don't ponder the human dimensions of the price that will be paid. After the war we might see casualty lists, but we ignore the emotional, mental and moral scars that will haunt people for decades to come.

In our class, however, we created a sacred space, a sanctuary, a place of safety. There, two dared to speak. It was the wounded ones who invited us into the deeper place of truth and mercy where hearts could begin to heal.

I have found many of the walking wounded around us, people whose scars are covered over by deep and sometimes hard layers of emotional armor. Some are children growing up with abuse. Some are warriors who never shared what they went through. Some are parents who buried their children. The traumas can be many, and they can even be scars we bear ourselves.

Can we create the safe place to open up? Can we risk speaking what we so often conspire together to suppress? Can we create communities of wounded healers? Such intentional healing is the only way to counter the damage done by the forgotten calculation.

CHAPTER 15

Unwrap the Grave Clothes!

SLIGHTLY MORE THAN a week before Easter, there was a resurrection. Jesus raised his friend Lazarus from the dead, claiming, "I am the Resurrection and the Life!" He had the stone rolled away from the tomb then shouted, "Lazarus, come out!" Lazarus came out, alive, but still wrapped tightly in the grave clothes. Jesus then commanded the stunned family and friends to unwrap the grave clothes to complete Lazarus' liberation from his bondage to death.

Grave clothes can come in many fashions. When a person comes to new life in faith, some of the rags of our old lives still cling to us. Old habits, old wounds, old bitterness, old self-limiting beliefs and old fears can still be wrapped around us, limiting our freedom of motion even though fresh new life courses through our spirits. Jesus gives us the task of unwinding one another's grave clothes.

I was doing a workshop in Central Asia and was able to help unwrap a 30-year-old winding sheet without even knowing it. I was teaching about taking nonviolent transforming initiatives from Jesus' Sermon on the Mount, dramatizing turning the other cheek, giving one's garment and going the second mile (see Matthew 5).

I was acting the role of the Roman soldier in occupied Judea and Galilee looking for someone to carry his pack. I'd picked out a certain person, but as I stepped toward her it seemed that God nudged me to a woman two seats over. I hadn't noticed her for the exercise, but in that half-second, suddenly I was pulling her to her feet and forcing her to carry my pack.

Author leading a workshop in Central Asia.

When we got to the end of the "first mile," I told her she had been listening to Jesus, so she took the lead going a "second mile." Instead of staying in the identity of victim, which I, as the Roman soldier, was giving her, she was claiming her own humanity by initiating her own action. She was the "gift-giver," offering help to someone who evidently needed her help. She turned the act of oppression against her to an act of kindness and generosity toward the oppressor.

After the break, she sought me out with a translator. We found a quiet place away from the other participants, and she told me her story. Thirty years ago, she had been victimized in a horrible way. She had forgiven the one who injured her so grievously, but she had felt guilty for getting into that situation. So often, victims of abuse end up despising themselves. She carried that self-hatred for 30 long years, even as her life developed and she became a pastor. There was still that hidden story wrapped tightly away in the grave clothes of self-loathing.

When I seized her, she was thrown back into that moment of oppression and abuse. Then she heard the echo of Jesus calling her to claim her humanity. In going the second mile, she could shuck off that winding sheet of self-hatred and claim her full being raised into the new life of God. Tears streamed down her radiant face as she told us what had happened. The "new creation" promised to the one who is "in Christ" was stepping out freely into the second mile of her life and ministry. The translator and I prayed for her, rejoicing with her and God for this new freedom she had found.

What old grave clothes still are wrapped around us? What old patterns and ways of thinking still hold us back? What old stories bind parts of us tightly? How will the healing word reach us to undo those constricting winding sheets so we can claim our full humanity in freedom?

CHAPTER 16

RefuJesus

I WAS STUNNED by the photo. It was a photo I'd captured while driving down the road with weary refugees walking along the berm. In the center of the photo was a family of three. The father was tall with a bundle on his head and a walking stick over one shoulder. The mother was also tall with a bundle on her head. Between them, holding his parents' hands, was a little boy, perhaps four years old. His stride was no match for his parent's long stride, so he must have been moving his smaller legs quite fast to just keep up. Their faces were etched with suffering. We were particularly taken by the boy's face. It was a face that knew hardship. His was not a childhood to be relished and treasured. I felt I was beholding the Holy Family.

∾

My wife and I had been in a van heading toward the church in Addis Ababa, Ethiopia, where we would be conducting a conflict transformation training. As we zipped along the road, we began passing hundreds of people walking toward the city.

Many of them had large bundles on their heads or backs. I asked our Ethiopian host what was going on, and he said these were refugees fleeing from the Ethiopia/Somalia border, where fighting had recently broken out.

I had an old simple film camera, and I quickly raised it and took a picture. We were traveling too fast and too close to the refugees to even guess at what I was shooting. I wouldn't know until I got home and had the film developed. In those days, it was too expensive to shoot off a bunch of pictures because you had to pay for every roll of film, for developing, and for printing the photos even if they turned out abysmal. So I just took one picture, and we continued on our way.

Author's photo of Somali refugees in Ethiopia.

When I got home and had the film developed, there was the stunning photo. I saw those three central figures as the Holy Family. Mary, Joseph, and Jesus looked like this family as they made their way back from Egypt to Nazareth. Following the visit of the Magi, they had fled the death squads of Herod the Great and gone to live in Egypt, likely in Alexandria, where there was a large Jewish community. After Herod's death, they returned to Nazareth, where Jesus grew up. Jesus was a toddler refugee like this little Ethiopian boy.

I'd seen the Holy Family once before in a New York subway tunnel. I'd just gotten off a train and was heading to the exit. There was a concrete alcove off the walkway where some homeless people were sleeping. I saw a couple trying to get settled in. The woman was pregnant and obviously near her time to give birth. There was no room in the Big Apple for this couple, except underground.

Boris Peterlin, a friend of mine from Croatia, wrote a book drawing from his experience covering the wars during the break-up of Yugoslavia. The book is titled *RefuJesus*. With exquisite art, the book merges the ancient story of Jesus as a child refugee and the experiences of all the displaced people in Croatia and Bosnia.

RefuJesus. What would our theology be like if we used Jesus' experience as a refugee as one of our foundational principles? What would our ethics and politics look like if Christians remembered that Jesus was an alien in a strange land, with his family fleeing violence? How would we treat the immigrants, the refugees, the homeless, and the displaced people in our midst?

Close-up of "the Holy Family" in Ethiopia.

The book *RefuJesus* by Boris Peterlin.

PART 4

Georgia Journeys

One of my favorite places to visit is the Republic of Georgia. Georgia is a beautiful country in the Caucasus Mountains. They have an incredible variety of scenery, wonderful food, excellent wine and hearty people. Georgia also has enough conflicts to keep peacemakers busy and to break their hearts. Here are only a few of the tales that come from a land I love.

CHAPTER 17

Just a Bit of Wood

LELA GAVE ME a gift smaller than a cell phone. I unwrapped it as she watched. It was a small piece of wood glued to a cross woven from twine, glued to a rectangular piece of cardboard, inserted into a thin plastic frame that perhaps was once the lid of a box. I was holding a piece of history.

I was in the Republic of Georgia in February 2004. I was part of a team consisting of the other Global Consultants for International Ministries as well as our Area Director. We were hosted by the Evangelical Baptist Church of Georgia, led by Bishop Malkhaz Songulashvili. We were treated to a grand tour of Georgia. We saw the medieval castle and Orthodox churches of Tbilisi; we climbed up to the desert monastery caves with decaying frescoes of centuries-old religious art; and we visited churches that had been under Soviet domination just a few years earlier.

But between the time that we set up our meeting and when we arrived in Georgia, a monumental event had shaken the country. A nonviolent revolution had ousted President Eduard

Shevardnadze. He had been popular in the U.S. as the foreign minister working alongside Soviet Premier Mikhail Gorbachev to bring in the new era of glasnost (openness) and perestroika (restructuring) that was rapidly followed by the collapse of the Soviet Union. For us, he was one of the good guys from the evil empire, but in Georgia, though he wasn't as bad as some leaders, he still allowed corruption and human rights abuses to go unchecked.

The Georgians were protesting a fraudulent election in the central square of Tbilisi. Mass protests built up in the streets. When President Shevardnadze tried to speak, (Parliament had been branded as illegitimate by the opposition) the demonstrators stormed the Parliament building and forced Shevardnadze to flee. The protesters were "armed" with red roses, thus giving the revolution its name, the Rose Revolution. Police refused to fire on the protesters and let them pass through their ranks into the Parliament building.

My friend Lela had been in the front row of the protesters. She was close to the opposition leader Mikheil Saakashvili, and whenever he was interviewed on TV it seemed that Lela was behind his shoulder. She faced the guns of the police and rushed into the Parliament building. She later took me and some other friends on a walking tour of the revolution as we all carried roses in remembrance of that day. But that was later.

During my first trip to Georgia in 2004, the dust of the revolution had barely settled. In late 2003, the Baptists played a part by serving hot drinks to the protesters in the rain as people shivered in the November chill under sheets of plastic. The Baptists had suffered at the hands of radical Orthodox militants who attacked their worship services, beaten many of their members and burned churches. One radical priest led the militants in reciting *The Lord's Prayer* as they burned Bibles and other literature in the Bible Society warehouse. These abuses brought the Baptists into the streets hoping for a government who would protect religious freedom and basic human rights. As our delegation traveled with the Baptist leaders, we sensed their excitement and expectation.

On our last full day in Georgia, our team led a conference. Each of us held workshops on our specialty. I had the largest group, as conflict was so much of their recent past and current concern. They had been living amid the swirl of historic events with no time to pause and reflect on

Georgians act out a skit about the Rose Revolution.

what happened and where they wanted to go next. This was their moment, not mine. My task was to simply allow them to do their own work.

I organized them into small groups. Since we were having trouble with translation, I asked each group to come up with a people sculpture or wordless skit about what the Rose Revolution meant to them. The energy was amazing as they found various ways to act out what happened and pour their feelings out using their bodies.

Then we harvested lists of what they achieved by the revolution, what they hoped to achieve that hadn't been accomplished yet and what was important that had not been addressed at all by the revolution. Tears streamed down my face as I heard them speak about the "birth of hope," and how they were participating in shaping their destiny for the first time in their lives.

We worked our way through some of the teaching of Jesus in the Sermon on the Mount, looking at what had happened through the lens of Jesus' call to take "transforming initiatives" (in the language of Glen Stassen). I felt like I had the front row seat to a retreat of nonviolent revolutionaries figuring out what happened and how to follow the ways of Jesus into a turbulent future.

Lela loved it! Lela lived on the cutting edge of the revolution's passion and relished the opportunity to take the time out to reflect and regroup for the ongoing work. She took the sheet of paper on which her small group had drawn a long-stemmed rose for their skit, had everyone sign it and presented it to me.

Workshop participants dramatize their march to the Presidential Office Building.

The rest of the delegation left Monday after a day of worship and celebration with the Baptists, but I stayed a few days extra because of air travel scheduling problems. Some problems are simply opportunities—Lela seized the opportunity. She arranged for me to meet for a couple days with some of her friends from the movement who were Baptist, Orthodox and secularists. We held a spontaneous two-day workshop on nonviolence.

At the end, Lela gave me her gift of the little piece of wood. When the protestors stormed Parliament, some rushed into Shevardnadze's office and threw his chair out the window. The chair smashed on the pavement below. Lela realized the broken

The framed splinter of Shevardnadze's chair.

remains of the chair were a piece of history, so she went outside and scavenged a leg and some bits left from the chair. She gave me one sliver in this humble, hastily crafted setting. It was her gift of history in appreciation for my gift of letting them reflect on the history they had made. Just a little bit of wood says so much and means so much.

CHAPTER 18

The New Rugged Cross

WHEN I WAS growing up, one of the favorite hymns sung in church was "The Old Rugged Cross." It spoke of the passionate love God had for us expressed in that cross. The cross was ugly, an instrument of death—yet so dear to those who, by faith, saw God's love on display. I saw two crosses in the Republic of Georgia that, together, told of faith and love that transformed something ugly into a message of hope.

The Orthodox Church was dominant in Georgia throughout its history and now is again since the breakup of the Soviet Union. In recent years, an extremist wing of the Orthodox Church has developed with leadership provided by radical militant priests. These radicals harassed and attacked Catholic and Protestant Christians. They blocked Muslims from gathering for Friday prayers and prevented houses of worship being built by other religious groups. Baptists in Georgia have been leading figures in the efforts for democracy and human rights, so they were frequently the target of some of these attacks.

In 2005, I went to Georgia with a group of young adults called the Xtreme Team. At one point in our trip, we visited Kakheti, a rural region northeast of Tbilisi, the capital. The local Baptists took us to a stone ruin in a village. It had been a Baptist church, but Orthodox radicals, under the leadership of a robed priest, burned down the house of worship.

As our team stepped inside the ruin, into what used to be the sanctuary, we discovered a cross. The cross was about eight feet high, formed of two scorched timbers that had been retrieved from the caved-in roof. Our team gathered around that blackened, rugged cross and prayed. We prayed for the congregation that had been driven from their church home. We prayed for those swept up in such hatred that they would engage in such an act against their neighbors. Afterward, our Kakheti Baptist hosts took us to a home to meet the rest of the congregation. We worshipped with them in that house.

Ruins of the Baptist church destroyed by Orthodox radicals.

A few years later I was back in Kakheti. My friend Merab Gaprindashvili, the Baptist bishop who had been a co-leader for the Xtreme Team, took me back to that church. We didn't go to the ruin, but to the new building in which the congregation was now meeting. In a wonderful act of ecumenical solidarity, an Anglican church in the United Kingdom helped the congregation purchase a farmhouse that had been remodeled into a sanctuary and educational facility.

In the sanctuary was a cross, what I named "the new rugged cross." It was handmade, with fresh blond wood sandwiching burnt wood salvaged from the old building. The altar in front of the cross was also made with both new wood and burnt wood. The cross and altar were a poignant reminder of the price people pay when religious militants violently repress those whose faith is different.

In that sanctuary, and in front of that new rugged cross, I was privileged to lead a workshop on dealing nonviolently and transformatively with persecution. We had members of four congregations present, all of whom experienced some form of attack from the Orthodox extremists. We

The cross made by burnt timbers from the torched church.

explored the situation of marginality and how to act positively in conflicts. We delved into biblical stories of how to find one's voice from the margins. We used a study from Esther 4 to see how Mordecai and Esther organized for change to save their people, applying the study to the issue of religious diversity and the persecution in Georgia.

Doing conflict transformation, training under the shadow of the new rugged cross spoke to me about hope amid suffering. The cross became a symbol for Christians of God's transforming power of love, bringing

The altar and cross made of new wood and the old burnt wood from the torched church.

new life out of death. God turned the cross of Jesus from an instrument of humiliation, torture and death into a divine gift of love, life and hope. Faith in that crucified and risen Christ transformed the suffering of that congregation into love and hope. They didn't meet the hatred of the radicals with their own bitterness and hatred. Instead, they let Christ's cross call them to love their enemies. For them, the fire of hate would not be allowed to have the last word. Rather, that last word would be of new beginnings through the power of love.

I'll never hear that old hymn again without the image of that new rugged cross in Georgia coming to mind.

CHAPTER 19

Contrasting Chapels

WE CAME THROUGH the door into a dark, round room. In the center was a circle of white pillars around a circular sunken space. In the center of the lowered floor was a white pedestal with a floodlight shining on it. There on the pedestal was a bronze death mask. It was the death mask of Joseph Stalin.

While traveling with colleagues in the Republic of Georgia, we visited the Stalin museum in Gori, the Georgian city where Stalin was born. During the days of the Soviet Union, the museum was one of the hottest tourist destinations in the Communist world. Now it was empty except for the exhibits and the curator.

The curator was a "true believer." She told us, "You have probably heard bad things about Stalin. But they (those who Stalin killed) were all criminals." Twenty million criminals. I shuddered as I listened to her parrot the line that justified the brutalities of one of the greatest mass murderers in human history.

The small house where Stalin was born under a colonnaded portico of the Stalin Museum.

Stalin was once one of the most powerful men on earth. We saw exhibits of his dominance and of the military might under his command. But the museum tour ended in a hushed chapel with the spotlight on a death mask. Stalin is no more, much to the joy and satisfaction of many and the regrets of a few.

A couple blocks down the street from the Stalin museum is the Gori Baptist Church. The small congregation first met in a house that was converted into a church. Baptists, along with people of all religions, were severely persecuted under Stalin's regime. In Aleksandr Solzhenitsyn's *One Day in the Life of Ivan Denisovich* about the Stalin-era gulag camps, one of the main and most positively intriguing characters is "the Baptist." But I didn't need a character in a novel to learn about the sufferings. My hosts were Georgian Baptists. One who took us through the museum said, "I always get the chills when I go by this place." We listened to older folks tell about the suffering they endured in those days and about all their

Our "true believer" guide at the Stalin Museum in Gori.

loved ones and friends who were exiled or who disappeared in the camps.

However, the church was very alive. Folks lined the benches to hear us. They sang with gusto in beautiful, plaintive Georgian tones. After the worship service, they set up tables and served a typical Georgian feast with plate upon overflowing plate filling the center of the tables. The homemade wine was brought out and proudly poured. *"Gaumarjos!"*—a toast to life, to love, to faith, to peace.

Stalin, who was once a bloody scourge upon the earth, ends his story with a death mask in a moldering museum. Meanwhile, the people he tried to extinguish are vibrant and joyous—a stone's throw from the place that marks the tyrant's birth. The Gori church also commemorates how a person died, but they believe that person came back to life. Whatever one may think about the resurrection of Jesus, that small Georgian Baptist congregation is a testimony to a power of life that has more durability than the power of death Stalin wielded.

Stalin's death mask.

CHAPTER 20

Protesting for Prayer

WE STOOD OUT in the hot sun in a square in downtown Tbilisi on a Friday afternoon. I was in my black, clerical robe, not the garb of choice out in a hot public square. But we were there for a reason: To demonstrate and bear witness to the right of everyone to pray as their religion and conscience might dictate.

I was there with a team of U.S. and Georgian young adults called IGNITE. We had been invited to join in this demonstration by the leaders of the Georgian Baptists. Three of their four bishops (unlike most Baptists around the world, the Georgians call their leaders bishops—and one, Rusudan Gotsiridze, is a woman) who were in the country at the time were present in their stunning purple robes. For them, this was a critical time to take a public stand—especially as Baptist Christians who advocate religious freedom for everybody.

A few weeks before, the extremists among the dominant Orthodox Church made global news when a few thousand of them, including robed priests and deacons, attacked an anti-homophobia demonstration in Tbilisi. There were less than a hundred demonstrators, but the Orthodox extremists rallied before the Parliament building and launched a brutal attack on them. People were chased into parks and shops and beaten. Police tried to rescue those they could and put them into police vans, which were then rocked by the angry mob. Our team flew into Georgia the day after that attack.

Bishop Merab Gaprindashvili was the local Baptist leader working with our team, but he became the leader of an ecumenical and interfaith committee that visited the Orthodox patriarch. The delegation included Catholic, Lutheran, Salvation Army, Pentecostal, Jewish and Muslim representatives; Merab was their spokesperson. (Imagine such a group in the U.S. gathering to speak out against violence against the LGBT community!) Most of the members of the delegation did not

Author holding a sign at the protest for prayer as Rusudan is interviewed by Georgian TV.

agree with the demonstrators, but they believed in their right to assembly, to voice their concerns and to be free from violence. The patriarch refused to denounce the radicals.

Both before and after the meeting, Merab met with our team at a café near the patriarch's offices. We talked about the rising violence and the free reign given to the extremists. That set the context for our three weeks in Georgia.

We didn't have to wait long for the next development. The first Friday we were in Georgia, we heard that the Orthodox radicals had blocked Muslims from gathering to pray in a village in eastern Georgia. There were confused and contra- dicting reports about how it happened, but the local imam ended up in the hospital. I

Demonstrators gather in downtown Tbilisi for the right to pray.

joined with the Baptist bishops in strategy discussions. Even- tually, we decided to wait and see what the government would do since they publicly asserted they would protect the right of the Muslims to gather for prayer.

Our team of young adults headed west with Merab to Batumi on the shores of the Black Sea. Batumi is the center of the strongest Muslim region in Georgia, very close to the bor- der of Turkey. Merab took us to the Georgian Muslims Union (GMU) offices. They hosted us for lunch, and we discussed the similar plights of Muslims and non-Orthodox Chris- tians in Georgia. The leader of the GMU gave us a tour of the Batumi mosque. Even though the mosque was so crowded for special occasions that worshippers would overflow onto the streets, the Muslim community was not allowed to build more mosques in this city. Before the Communists took over, there had been multiple mosques. However, they were either destroyed or converted for other purposes. Now even those old mosques could not be replaced.

We returned to Tbilisi with a deeper understanding of the Muslim community in Georgia and were greeted with the news that the Muslims in eastern Georgia were barred from gathering for prayer once again. The government had done nothing. The Baptist leaders and others upholding religious freedom called for a demonstration the next Friday.

That evening, I gathered the IGNITE team together to talk about the invitation to join in the demonstration for the freedom to pray. The memories of what happened to the anti-homophobia demonstrators were vivid to us. I told the young team members that because of my involvement with the Georgian Baptists over the years, I had to join them at the demonstration. But this was not something that any of them signed up for.

As we discussed the historic Baptist principles of freedom of conscience and freedom of religion, every team member insisted that they wanted to be a part of the demonstration—even if threatened by the Orthodox radicals. We did a short training in nonviolent action and prepared ourselves for various scenarios. What

Author listens as a Muslim shares his appreciation for the demonstrators.

could team members do if they felt it was too dangerous for them? How and where would we all meet afterward? None of our team members had ever participated in a demonstration of any kind before. This would be their baptism into activism.

On Friday, we met Rusudan and her family down near the square. We brought poster board and markers and began to make signs in both Georgian and English. At noon various demonstrators began to gather—Catholics, Jews, Pentecostals and Yazidis; there were no Orthodox leaders, but many disenchanted and dismayed Orthodox young people; and us Baptists—me in my black robe and the Georgian Baptist bishops in their purple robes. There were about a hundred of us, and we were surrounded by perhaps a hundred police in riot gear.

We kept vigil in the square nearest the Tbilisi mosque for a while. Georgian media crews interviewed all the Baptist bishops—they were the only religious leaders dressed in clearly identifiable clergy garb. Rusudan and I held a sign saying "LOVE YOUR NEIGHBOR." Rusudan had become a national figure in discussions about religious tolerance and freedom, so the TV news crews came to interview her while I stood there and smiled.

One Orthodox radical arrived in a black robe. His eyes were hard and hate-filled, staring daggers at us. That was the greatest threat that showed up.

After a while, the demonstrators decided to march up a few blocks to the mosque. Rusudan and I were in the front row leading the way. When we got to the mosque, all the Muslims there were still at prayer. The demonstrators faced the mosque with their signs, but I told them to face out. We weren't speaking to the Muslims at the mosque; rather, we were standing together to protect them and their right to pray. Our signs were for the larger community.

When prayers were over, the Muslim men came out to find the street in front of the mosque jammed with demonstrators. From previous visits, I knew that the Muslims had a higher percentage of English speakers than Georgians on the streets of Tbilisi, so I began talking with them about what had happened. All of them knew about the Muslims being blocked from their prayers by Orthodox radicals. But their imam, who knew about the demonstration, had not told his congregation what was happening. I shared with the Muslim men about what we were doing and why. Their fear was replaced with appreciation. One young man was very moved, so he gave a spontaneous speech of appreciation to the demonstrators. His words were the perfect conclusion to our day.

Standing up for our rights is important. The bigger challenge is to stand up for the rights of others. Dr. Martin Luther King, Jr. once said, "Injustice anywhere is a threat to justice everywhere." Baptists in Georgia had experienced discrimination and violence from the Orthodox radicals. But when their Muslim neighbors and their gay and lesbian neighbors were the targets, they took the lead to stand in solidarity for justice for everyone. Do we struggle for only our freedom, or for the freedom for everyone?

PART 5

Voices Matter

*One of the major themes in our conflict transformation train-
ing is supporting voices being raised from the margins. Without
such voices, change for the better will seldom happen. Voices
from the margins usually have something to teach us. Here are
some of the voices I have heard.*

CHAPTER 21

"Let Me Speak!"

"**LET ME SPEAK!**" The small black African man held his ground. He had stood up at a conference question and answer time and begun to talk "off topic." As his statement went on, the moderator tried to cut him off. Finally, exasperated the man made a simple demand: "Let me speak!"

"Let me speak!" was the message that resonated most powerfully with me during the Global Baptist Peace Conference held in Rome, Italy in February 2009. The message was not delivered in a plenary address or sermon. It was not on the program. It did not come from one of the significant global peacemaking figures we had arranged as plenary speakers.

Rather, this message erupted during a question and answer period following the plenary presentation by Gustavo Parajon. (Gustavo was from Nicaragua, a pastor and medical doctor who played a key mediation role in ending the war in Nicargua—one of my greatest heroes.) The Rev. Sini Ngindu Bindanda, a Baptist pastor from Congo who served an immigrant church in Milan, got up to ask a question, which turned into a long statement about the war in Congo. Rev. Bindanda was well spoken but clearly not responding to Gustavo's presentation.

The moderator finally tried to cut him off and press for the question. Rev. Bindanda kept making his point. The moderator then approached the microphone to take it away. Rev. Bindanda then said clearly and firmly, "Let me speak!" He was proud, gentle and yet insistent. He continued on, determined to say what he wanted to say. Finally the moderator gave up and let him finish.

After Rev. Bindanda concluded, Gustavo responded with his own eloquent wisdom about what had just happened. He said that one of the most important things for people from small countries (perhaps small in terms of global power, not necessarily geographic size) is the need to find a voice. This Congolese pastor raised his voice and was determined to have his say. What he said was something we needed to hear, as the war in Congo was the bloodiest on the planet since World War II—yet it got very little attention, even in a peace conference! Rev. Bindanda's voice was speaking out for the millions of voiceless from one of the most marginalized places in the world.

Raising the voices from the margins proved to be a critical part of that conference in Rome. So often, I have taught alone or with colleagues about mainstreams and margins. We study stories from the Bible and then share stories from our histories about people from incredibly marginalized positions finding the courage and creativity to raise their voices. Nonviolent direct action has often made this possible. Again and again, I've seen the margins stand up across the world and raise their powerful voices demanding attention, demanding justice and demanding peace.

When a voice is raised from the margin near us, we have a choice. We can act like the moderator and try to maintain proper order, our order. Or, we can be like Gustavo Parajon.

He didn't relate from his position as a big global peace figure who was famous enough to be a conference plenary speaker. Instead, he connected to his experience at the margin, being from a small country that knows what it is like to be beaten up by bigger powers and ignored in its travails. He heard the voice from the margin with ears sensitized by his own marginal experiences. He supported and affirmed the right of the margin to speak, helping to create enough space for the voice to be heard. We all have that place within us that can awaken our empathy so we can hear the voices crying out around us.

CHAPTER 22

Voice From the Empty Chair

I PLACED AN empty chair at the front of the sanctuary where we were holding the conflict transformation training. Above the chair was a sign "Ngoroko," which means "Warrior." That was the name given by the group for a fictional Pokot young man who had been killed in the cattle rustling conflicts that plague this area of northern Kenya. The chair was for his "mother." What would she say?

Suddenly, a woman walked to the front, sat in the chair and began to speak.

༄

A friend named Pini Kidulah invited me to the Pokot region of Kenya to lead a three-day conflict transformation training. While studying in the U.S., Pini attended a 10-day training I run for peacemaking leaders who want to do the kind of work I do. She went back home to do peace work as well as empower women through her organization, called Jitokeze. Pini invited me to come and lead training sessions.

She briefed me on the particular conflicts and cultures of the area. Pokot culture in the rural areas is based on cattle.

One's wealth and status is determined by how many head of cattle you own. To get a bride, a young man needs to give 20 or 30 cattle to the bride's father, but a young person is likely to only own two or three cows at most. So how does one get the needed cows to get a bride? They steal them. However, everyone is armed with automatic weapons. Young men have been slaughtered in terrible numbers from cultural values and mandates that call for cattle rustling.

Pokots generally have done little to acknowledge those killed in the cattle conflicts. Many dead are left unburied out of fear of evil sprits. Life goes on, and the fighting goes on, as if nothing happened. Grief is never acknowledged or dealt with; rather, all that happened and any resulting feelings are ignored or repressed. Pini and I discussed a number of ways to approach this topic. But even as the day when we'd deal with trauma in conflict began, I still wasn't sure what to do.

We began with the biblical story of Rizpah in 2 Samuel 21. Rizpah was a mother who lost two sons to political violence carried out in the name of religion. She took up a nonviolent vigil over the bodies of her sons. After many months, her action finally moved King David, who ordered the killings, to repentance. There were other characters in the story that experienced trauma and handled it in various, nonproductive ways. We role-played various parts of the story, interviewing people in the roles of the biblical characters. The Rizpah story was always a powerful and climactic moment in our trainings, but I wanted to move toward a direct application in the Pokot context.

I asked participants to talk about what happens when someone is killed in cattle rustling conflicts. Various men spoke out about issues of revenge or compensation depending on who did the killing and where the killing took place. They went on for a while, trying to make sure I caught all the nuances about their process to determine the appropriate response. But no women spoke. I sensed a significant gap between the men and the women on this issue, so I invited a woman to speak. One of the women chiefs spoke (they had many women in chief roles), but she sounded just like the men. We were getting nowhere. It was time for what we in the field of experiential education call "emergent design"—also known as flying by the seat of your pants, or making it up as you go.

I decided to make the discussion more concrete, so I invited them to name an imaginary young man who was killed rustling cattle. They chose to name him Ngoroko, "Warrior." I wrote Ngoroko on the flip chart paper at the front of the room. Then I placed a chair under the name and invited the participants to think about what Ngoroko's mother might say if she were here.

Instead, an older woman came forward, sat in the chair, and began to speak. She told of her pain and sadness. She told about the sadness that more people would die because of the death of her son. She told of her loneliness. She was unable to receive support and comfort from the community,

Pokot woman who spoke from the empty chair.

something she longed for. There was no talk of revenge or compensation. Instead she spoke of her pain and a desire that no more killing take place. Her face reflected her message—grim, somber and etched with anguish.

Then, as a group, we talked about culture and how cultures change. No culture is static, but people are faced with new challenges that force them to come up with new solutions that reflect cultural values and transform the situation. We can face choices about enduring the limiting behaviors made normative, or we can choose a better way for ourselves, reshaping our culture in the process. What was defined as "Pokot culture" was actually an expression of the men's values. The Pokot women were silent and isolated, except the female chief who spoke out of the same context and power setting of the men. But when an ordinary Pokot woman spoke, a mother, she revealed how the cultural ways of dealing with death by violence were inadequate. She challenged her contemporaries even as Rizpah challenged the people of her time.

At the break, I made a beeline for this woman. She said she was able to get into the role of Ngoroko's mother because her aunt lost a son in the violence. Another woman entered our conversation. She expressed that she wanted to speak in the chair and tell of the loss of her two sons but knew she would break down if she spoke. She deeply appreciated how we dealt with the topic and the challenge to face up to the cost of violence upon their families and society.

After the break, we explored creative ways of recognizing victims of violence that lead to healing and reconciliation rather than perpetrating cycles of violence. The idea of planting trees met with a lot of enthusiasm. The next day, Pini arranged for us to plant trees in memory of the dead and in hope for the new life these trees would sustain. The tree-planting was a joyous time, allowing an affirmation of a hopeful vision rather than the calculations about appropriate levels and means of revenge.

Much of peacemaking is about supporting the voices that are drowned out in the rages of violence. The Pokot mothers had been intimidated into silence. They were part of the culture, but their voices were muted by social pressure. The woman who filled that empty chair with her presence and her voice opened a creative opportunity for change. These voices from the margins can sometimes bring us the words of wisdom we need in order to see the cost of our violent ways and point us to better behavior and healing actions.

CHAPTER 23

"What You Are Saying Is Worthless!"

"WHAT YOU ARE saying is worthless!" That is not what you like to hear from a participant when you are leading a workshop, but that is exactly what was said when Daniel Hunter and I were leading a conflict transformation training in one of the ethnic minority regions of Myanmar.

Daniel and I had been leading a series of trainings in the capital, Yangon, and into the northern part of the country. The military dictatorship had a firm grip on the country. Some of the ethnic minority groups had insurgencies fighting the central government. Other ethnic insurgencies had entered into cease-fires but were frustrated because the cease-fires did not address any of the underlying conditions in the conflicts. The democracy movement was dormant within the country following severe repression. Fear stalked the land.

Our workshops were very participatory, which led to two difficulties for us as facilitators. First, everyone was fearful of the military, so most people were hesitant to say anything in a workshop. Participants had a very small "comfort zone," and it wasn't a big step to their "alarm zone" where their only concern was self-preservation. Second, in Myanmar there is a high respect for the teacher. The teacher must always be right, so nobody would challenge anything we said. If we tried to elicit the opinions and ideas of participants, they would try to wait to hear what Daniel and I thought before venturing out their own comments in line with the words of the revered teachers. As a result, Daniel and I were frustrated as we continued to encourage participation.

We had traveled to the northern regions of Myanmar, where there had been a long history of vicious combat between the Myanmar army and ethnic insurgents. Many times, civilians were swept up in the violence, causing people to flee across borders into China or Thailand. In this setting, Daniel and I were teaching about conflict resolution—getting to win-win solutions—and nonviolence.

As we were in the part of the workshop exploring nonviolence, one participant stood up and said with great fervor, "What you are saying is worthless! The army will just come and kill us all, so what you are saying is of no value at all!"

(From left) Author and Daniel Hunter leading a workshop in Myanmar.

Daniel was leading at that particular point in the training, and he was taken aback by this devastating rejection of what we were doing. He turned to me for help. I didn't know what to do either, so I "noodled"—what musicians do when they are between songs, stringing notes somewhat together to fill the time. I can't recall anything I said because I wasn't really saying anything.

Meanwhile, Daniel was taking the time and space to think about what occurred and figure out what to do. When he was ready, he gave me a sign. I threw the facilitation back to Daniel. Daniel pointed at the man who had critiqued us and, in a voice matching his, demanded, "What gives you the strength to criticize us? We are the teachers! What inside of you gives you the strength to challenge us?"

The man was initially shocked at Daniel's response. Then, he realized Daniel wasn't attacking him at all but was trying to dig deeper. Daniel talked about the culture of respecting the teacher in Burma, and how nobody had questioned us about anything. Yet here was this one person going against the cultural tide and making a devastating critique of what we were doing. How could he do that? What was happening inside him that enabled him to speak out with such power?

Soon, the man was engaged with Daniel about what was going on inside himself. He was angry about the repression. He was angry about the constant violence. He was frustrated at his inability to act, and his anger was not just at the situation but also at how helpless and powerless he felt. He couldn't see that what we were saying could match the power of the feelings he had in the face of the massive problems he lived with every day. That's where his verbal explosion had come from.

Daniel thanked him for giving voice to these powerful feelings. For the rest of the workshop, Daniel and I affirmed the anger at the injustice and violence people faced. We worked at how to turn anger into positive energy for nonviolent transformative responses to the situations they lived with. This man and his feelings became the key point of interaction for us throughout the rest of that workshop. He even stayed for two hours afterward as we explored issues deeper with a small cluster of other participants hanging about because of the excitement and energy of the discussion.

Sometimes, we are afraid of the anger and the energy of others. Daniel and I certainly had a first response of confusion and panic. But anger can be a very constructive energy source if it can be acknowledged, owned and channeled in creative ways. Anger lets us know something is seriously wrong. Anger can provide the motivation and drive for change. The key is not always to look at where the anger is directed, but rather at where the anger is coming from. Going deeper, or "peeling the onion" of our emotions, can get us to the inner foundation from which powerful action can be constructed.

Months later, Daniel was back in that region and talked to some of the people involved in that training. An incident had happened where the Burmese army acted in a repressive way. The people had stood up to the army using some of the methods we had covered in our workshop, standing up for their needs in a firm but nonviolent way. The army commander agreed to work with them and an acceptable solution was reached. The workshop participants were ecstatic because this was the first time they had ever successfully and peacefully stood up for themselves and achieved their goals.

CHAPTER 24

The Bolivian Way?

I WAS IN Bolivia at a historic moment. Evo Morales had recently become president. He was the first indigenous person to become president of a country in the Americas. Bolivia was full of pride among indigenous people and fearful uncertainty among Bolivians of Spanish ancestry. What would be next? How would Bolivia and this new president deal with the issues of diversity and power?

I'd been invited to conduct a series of conflict transformation workshops for Protestant churches throughout the country during this historic moment. We started at Santa Cruz in the lowlands, then worked our way up to Cochabamba, and finally to the capital, La Paz, and the neighboring city of El Alto.

El Alto is a city of around a million people sprawling on the high plateau that runs longways through the Andes Mountains. The edge of El Alto overlooks La Paz, which is set in a massive bowl and surrounded by the plateau on one side and towering Andes peaks the rest of the way. At around 15,000 feet, La Paz is the highest capital in the world.

Our workshops in El Alto and La Paz discussed the theme of dealing well with our diversity and used the terminology of "mainstream" and "margins." We had quite a bit of diversity in the group. Most of the participants were men, pastors in suits. Some of the women wore traditional costumes of the Aymara, colorful dresses and a bowler hat.

The opening exercise for the workshop section on diversity was "Tape on the Forehead." We put small pieces of masking tape with various colored designs on people's foreheads. Participants are then instructed to "form into groups" without using words. Most people form into groups based on the design on the tape on their foreheads, using sign language to communicate about the tape they see, often aided by emerging leaders.

At this workshop, three local women formed their own group. As everyone else milled around to find their groups, the women stood contentedly to the side. Soon a man noticed them. He came over and broke up the group of women. He escorted each of them to a group that had a matching design on their forehead. Once everyone was settled, we began debriefing.

I invited a conversation about what happened. People shared about the process of finding others who had the same sign on their forehead, about people who came and guided them to the right group. Everyone was happy to be in a group. Meanwhile, the women were quiet.

Finally, I asked if anyone had noticed the group of women who had formed at the beginning of the exercise. Oh yes, they had been noticed. Then the participants spoke about how someone went over and helped the women find their correct group. One of the men said, "This is the Bolivian way," perhaps meaning helping people out to find the place they should be. The women were still quiet.

I asked if anybody asked the women what they thought about this. Nobody had. So we invited them to speak. They were not happy about what had happened. They had enjoyed being in their own group with their other women friends. They didn't want to join the groups they had been forced into. They had been sullenly quiet because of how they felt. I suggested that maybe this hadn't been the Bolivian way, but rather the Bolivian "men's" way. All the women agreed with that! They were Bolivians, too, and they felt their desires as women had been completely overlooked. Even the men understood and agreed that they had made assumptions and acted against the wishes of the women.

I asked the group to go deeper and think about how their awareness had changed. A few moments earlier, everyone who was speaking was in agreement that the right thing had been done in breaking up the women and getting them to the "proper" group with the same forehead sign. Now everyone was in agreement that their action hadn't been just, because the interests of the women had been completely ignored and overridden. I asked about this realization.

For about 10 minutes everyone was silent pondering what had just happened. How did awareness change? Awareness didn't change until the women spoke out. What enabled the women to speak out? In this case, someone in the mainstream in a dominant position—namely me as workshop leader—noticed what was happening and created a safe place for the voice of the women to be raised. The women were margins in this group as well as in Bolivian society. These particular women remained silent, even when they felt misused. But when the opportunity came and an invitation to speak was given, they spoke their minds!

Change seldom comes from the top down in ways that empower or support the margins. Almost always, change happens because the margins find a way to speak out and stand for their needs and their rights. The dominant mainstream is usually clueless about the experiences at the margin, as the Bolivian men were about the women. We even make assumptions that "our way" is everyone's way. "It's the Bolivian way" wasn't true. We were seeing the Bolivian men's way. The

Bolivian men changed their understanding once they heard the voice of the Bolivian women.

These dynamics are true in every group because the people in it are different. There is a mainstream within each group that gives the group its identity and shapes the culture for the group. Then there are the margins, the alternatives to the mainstream. How voices are raised from the margins and how well mainstreams listen to and respond to those voices determines the capacity for growth in the group.

Interestingly, this little exercise gave an insight for the calling for Protestant churches during this historic moment in Bolivian history. Catholics had been in the religious mainstream, and many Protestants had been victims of severe persecution and even martyrdom. Baptists chose to be silent in the larger society to the point of passing a policy statement to never speak out about political or social issues. Newly elected President Evo Morales was holding a constitutional convention to deal with the issue of diversity in the country. He invited all minorities, including religious minorities, to participate. Would the Baptists participate? Through the exercise, they saw that they could be a voice for those in the margins because so many of the margins were in their congregations—not just religious margins—but women and various ethnic groups. They could use their place at the constitution convention to support the voices from the margins and thus help Bolivia to grow as a nation.

When we are in the margins, do we tend to be silent or speak out? If we speak out, do we do it in a way that helps people to hear us or to become defensive? When we are in the mainstream, are we even aware of what is happening in the margins? When voices come from the margins, do we listen to see what we can learn? If we can interact with each other constructively and with respect in both the mainstream and the margins, our group will be able to grow.

PART 6

Words Matter

Not only do voices matter, but what we say with those voices matters. Words have meaning in themselves. Words also have meaning that shift with their context. Words can give life or take it away.

CHAPTER 25

Jesus Speaks Mapudungun

I LOOKED AT Lucy, a Mapuche woman in our Chile workshop. I told her that when she gets to heaven Jesus is not going to say *"Bienvenidos!"* Rather Jesus will open his arms and say, *"Mari mari!"* Lucy's eyes welled with tears and her face shone. It was the most emotionally charged moment of the workshop. Jesus speaks Mapudungun, and without a Spanish accent.

Does Jesus speak Mapudungun? Some churches have evidently thought not. The Mapuche are indigenous people of Chile, a people never conquered by the Incas but incorporated into Chile by the Spanish colonizers. They have a spiritually based culture, so some of the early missionaries and even some of the Protestant churches consider anything associated with the Mapuche culture as pagan. Many Mapuche, in coming to Christ, abandoned their culture and tried to acclimate themselves to the dominant Spanish-based culture. The use of Mapudungan, the Mapuche language, has been eroded by direct repression and simple disuse due to assimilating into the majority culture.

This is not just a Chilean problem. Back in the 19th century U.S., many mission schools of various denominations sought to educate Native Americans. But part of their mission was intentionally to extinguish the indigenous culture that was viewed as "pagan." Students were forbidden to speak their tribal language. Their names were replaced with "Christian" English names. They were kept away from their families that conveyed such culture.

Language can be a key matter for both identity and justice. Who we are is incorporated into language issues. We speak of the "mother tongue," the language and worldview developed in our most intimate and primary relationship. We have our "heart language," the way we speak when we are expressing our deepest self. What is the default way we give voice to who we are, what we aspire to, and the thoughts that grow from our deepest passions? Taking away one's own language as an act of oppression that goes to the very core of our humanity.

Lucy (center) with other workshop participants.

In most of Chile, the Mapuche were being squeezed into the dominant Spanish-speaking Chilean culture. In some places, there was a strong religious endorsement of Mapuche cultural extinction. But things had been stirring in the Mapuche heartland. Conflict is brewing to affirm, reclaim and restore their identity.

Mapuche activists responded to the prejudice they experienced with pride, anger and violence. Tensions began to build between the Mapuche and the dominant culture. People were killed, homes were burned and land was occupied by the activists. The government responded with force. One of my missionary colleagues, Dwight Bolick, worked in Chile along with his wife, especially among the Mapuche. They did development work and other outreach projects with the churches in central Chile, in Temuco, Panguipulli and surrounding areas. Dwight invited me to come to Chile to equip the churches—both Mapuche and Spanish-speaking Chilean—for conflict transformation work in this developing context of confrontation.

As I listened to the stories of the workshop participants, I learned about the loss of language. We trained about the dynamics of mainstreams and margins in groups. It was clear that the Mapuche were experiencing serious marginalization, and language was a key touch point. I heard how the denial of Mapudungun was often encouraged and even enforced in some church settings.

I learned the Mapuche greeting, *"Mari mari."* At one point in the workshop I looked at Lucy, a Mapuche woman and seminary student who had been very engaged in the discussion. When I told her that Jesus would greet her in heaven with a hearty *"Mari mari"* her eyes welled with tears and her face shone. Jesus speaks

Author speaks to Lucy during an exercise in the conflict transformation training.

Mapundungun, Lucy's mother tongue, her heart language, and he does so without a Spanish or English accent.

There is firm biblical ground for that affirmation. The Bible says in Revelation 7:9 that there will be "*a great multitude that no one can count, from every nation, from all tribes and peoples and languages, standing before the throne and before the Lamb.*" Mapudungun will be one of those languages in heaven. God's glory can't be fully expressed without the sound of Mapudungun, however marginalized and disparaged that language may have been on earth. Every heart language and every mother tongue has a place in the marvelous sonic symphony of heaven. That heavenly vision influences how we envision and enact justice on earth.

Conflict transformation requires respecting the humanity and the voices of those at the margins. Sometimes, out of anger and frustration, the voice from the margins is raised through violence. Such expressions from the margins usually become counterproductive, destroying lives and property, leading to deep alienation and trauma and allowing mainstreams to justify their own repressive violence for the sake of law and order. I saw that dynamic at work in Chile with the government's heavy-handed response to the violence and occupations of Mapuche activists. We have seen the same dynamic in Ferguson, Missouri where police looking like U.S. Marines responded with overwhelming force to the anger of young blacks over the killing of an unarmed black man by police.

Listening to the voices from the margins is necessary for learning what is going on, where the pains are, and what the needs and concerns are. We need to hear from both the margins and the mainstreams to gain the information needed to come up with creative solutions. Jesus can speak Mapudungun and hear that heart language. I can't understand it—but if I work at listening, even with a translator, I can hear the Mapuche heart. Hearing the heart's expressions from the margins is a vital step toward peace.

CHAPTER 26

"Jesus Is Super!"

"*JEZUS JEST* **SUPER!**" the graffiti read, painted over a heart. Jesus is super, I agree, except the place where this "witness" was scrawled was the wall of a Jewish synagogue. "Jesus is super!" became nauseating blasphemy.

We were in the Jewish ghetto of Krakow, Poland. The Isaac (or Izaak) Synagogue had once been a major place of worship for the Jews of Krakow, but the German Nazis deported the entire community to the concentration camps where most died in appalling misery. Many were gassed in the death camp in Auschwitz, which sprawls as a monstrous memorial less than an hour's drive from Krakow. The Isaac Synagogue houses a photographic memorial of the deportation, suffering and deaths of Krakow's Jews. Had the graffiti artist who thought Jesus was super visited that exhibit?

In Warsaw, we saw many cinema marquees advertising Mel Gibson's *The Passion of the Christ,* which came out at that time. I am deeply moved in my spirit when I think of the sufferings of Jesus for our salvation, but I am also deeply grieved that many Christians are still insensitive to the way some who call themselves Christians have used Jesus' death to stir the fires of anti-Semitism. Gibson's extra-biblical script additions about Pontius Pilate lessen Roman culpability in Jesus' death, awakening both ancient and recent memories and fears among Jews.

This is an old issue. In Prague I read the history, which goes back hundreds of years, of the Jews periodically being driven from their homes and murdered in the name of Christ. There is a beautiful cross on the Charles Bridge that has a golden Hebrew insult to the Jewish community across it. The Holocaust was not an aberration, just a more efficient and methodical expression of the bigotry expressed in so many chapters of Western history.

The Isaac Synagogue in Krakow.

This is a current issue. Anti-Semitism is on the rise in Europe along with acts of violence against immigrants. When we visited the memorial sites related to the heroic Jewish uprising in the Warsaw Ghetto in 1943, I was grieved to find "*Juden raus!*" ("Jews out!" in German) painted on the memorial stone over the ruin of Mila 18, the uprising command post.

I believe that Jesus is super, but how to we appropriately make that witness? Do we give our testimony in film or graffiti clueless of the echoes of old horrors we trigger by our insensitivity?

In Poland, my wife, Sharon, and I were blessed to see a super witness growing among the Baptists in the wake of the fall of communism. Sharon and I were invited to be leaders for the first-ever social ministries conference for the Polish Baptist Union. Forty people gathered at a

Sign about the memorial exhibit at the Isaac Synagogue.

seminary in Rodość from cities across Poland to share what they were doing as expressions of God's love and to explore ways to strengthen their ministries. We learned of ministries to children, many of the "economic orphans" lost amid the turbulent transition from communism to capitalism. We met a young couple that prepared 650 sandwiches each morning for homeless people in their city. We met a healthcare administrator who runs a special summer camp for children from Ukraine and Belarus stricken from the radiation of the Chernobyl disaster. We met people who care for the frail elderly whose pensions dissolved with the collapse of the communist state. Then, after the conference we were guided by Polish Baptists who told the story of Polish Jews with empathy that spoke more of the love of Jesus than graffiti ever could.

International work often involves translation. Sharon was learning Polish; she was told the first 10 years are the hardest! Poles would joke that Polish is the language of heaven because it takes an eternity to master it. Translating the love of God needs more than words. Acts are also necessary. Loving action is what we see in Jesus. Loving action is what we see when people act out their faith in deeds of mercy, justice and compassion. When Christians translate the Gospel into demonstrations of love, then the words "Jesus is super!" will have a context and content that is truly good news.

CHAPTER 27

My Chinese Name

I HAVE A Chinese name! It was given to me by Jonathan Chan in Hong Kong. I can't write the characters in this manuscript, so you'll have to follow in Roman script. In Putonghua, the official language of China, sometimes called Mandarin, my name is Deng Bai Li. In Cantonese, the language spoken in Hong Kong, the name is Dan Bak Lei.

The first syllable "Deng" or "Dan" is a common surname (remember the former premier Deng Xiao Ping?), and it sounds close to my English name. The second syllable "*Bai*" or "*Bak*" means "hundred." The third syllable "*Li*" or "*Lei*" means "gains." The last two names together, literally "hundred gains," mean "lots of benefits" or "everything is fine."

Jonathan Chan attended my conflict transformation training in Hong Kong in March 2005. He later extended an invitation for me to return and conduct more training among the churches in Hong Kong. As we were making the plans, he said I needed a Chinese name. In giving me the name Dan

Bak Lei he said, "It is very much related to your objectives in conflict transformation where you want to arrive at win-win solutions that benefit all parties and make everything fine for everyone involved.

Taking a name from another language is common in Hong Kong. Many people are given a Chinese name by their family. Then, in school, they choose or are given an English name, such as "Jonathan," that they will use in many of the contexts in education, business and multicultural social

Author teaching about win/ win solutions in Hong Kong.

affairs. I personally like to learn people's Chinese names as I feel the use of English names gives in to and accommodates American laziness at learning names of people from different cultures. However, I do appreciate that in Hong Kong most individuals pick a name that they like, perhaps because of its meaning or because it sounds close to their given name. In much of the racist past of the U.S., slaves brought from Africa and Native Americans were given "Christian" names in mission schools, sometimes only first names, or sometimes the last name of their slave owner. No choice was involved. People were robbed of their identity as they were forced to assume the identity given by their oppressors.

Jonathan asked my permission to give me a Chinese name. The process Jonathan used was one of deep integrity, both to think of the sound of my given name and the meaning of the Chinese words in relation to who I was as a person and to my life's work. So this name was not a robbery but an affirmation.

In Revelation 2:17, Jesus speaks about those who overcome receiving a "*new name that no one knows except the one who receives it.*" What does that mean? I'm not certain. But I suspect it includes a meaning that captures the essence of who we are as persons or what our lives have been about in God's redeeming work. Jesus gave Simon a new name, "Cephas" or "Peter," which in Aramaic and Greek respectively means "rock." Peter is the rock because "*on this rock I will build my church.*" It was a prophetic name that saw past Peter's failure in denying Jesus to the man he would become after Pentecost.

Maybe my name in heaven will be Chinese—Dan Bak Lei. If not, Jonathan did a service in giving me a name that captures the spirit I try to live out.

What would you like captured in a name that would signify the essence of who you are and what your life is about?

PART 7

The Art of Peacemaking

Unlike a few decades ago, there are now many courses of study and degree programs in peace, conflict resolution, and conflict transformation. However, peacemaking is not a matter of social engineering. Peacemaking is not a technique to be practiced. The actual work of peacemaking is often an art in which turning points come through actions or words that are completely unplanned. The peace artist is able to recognize the particular moment pregnant with a new possibility and to act as a midwife to the birth of that possibility in a conflict situation. I occasionally practice that art, but I also study some of the masters.

CHAPTER 28

Peace Games

I GREW UP in a military family. I spent most of my childhood and youth on military bases. One of my favorite memories was off the base, when I was swept up in a military exercise. I was on a Boy Scout camping trip with our troop from the base. We were doing winter camping in a local state park at the same time that an ROTC unit from a nearby university was engaged in war games. As we hiked during the day, we saw the student troops staging their maneuvers and firing blanks when they were engaged in simulated combat. That night our camp shelter was "attacked." Smoke bombs went off around us, and we "civilians" were captured. It was a trill as a teenager. Unlike war, this was a game.

The military is very good at games. They are called war games, and they serve specific educational purposes. War games are run so soldiers learn new ways of analyzing situations and battlefields. War games enable soldiers to learn new skills and put them into practice. War games also help soldiers develop more effective and efficient ways of working together.

Peacemakers can learn from the pedagogy of the military. We can use games to help activists analyze situations and the "lay of the land." We can use games to teach skills and provide practice in new behaviors. Games can provide the opportunity to develop better teamwork for accomplishing group goals. But instead of using games to learn the ways of war, we use them to learn the ways of peace.

Participants in the soccer match at the Naga peace talks in Chiang Mai.

Many of the activities peace trainers use are "peace games." We have our "toolbox" of such games—children's games with special twists, simple or incredibly complex simulations or role-plays, group challenges. But I saw one master peacemaker take the most popular game in the world and turn it into a peace game par excellence!

Wati Aier is the founder and principal of the leading Baptist seminary in Nagaland in northeast India, and he has been the convener of the Forum for Naga Reconciliation (FNR) that has facilitated peace processes between Naga insurgent groups. We worked together in a series of peace and reconciliation talks held in Chiang Mai, Thailand. The talks were stalled in a cycle of frustration and mutual recrimination about acts of violence back in Nagaland. Many of us, both on the international team supporting the process and the Naga civil society leaders on the FNR, were growing frustrated and coming up with little creative.

As we were preparing to begin a new round of talks, Wati came to the international team facilitating some of the process and announced, "We're going to play football!" (What we in the U.S. call soccer is called football in most of the world.) I was shocked at the idea. We had so little time, and the tension was too high for dawdling around with games in our free time. But Wati insisted. In fact, he had already told the factional leaders, some of whom had taken off to the local mall to buy athletic shoes for the match. He was the one who had convened the peace process, so against our better judgment we gave in to his plan for the day.

Wati was definitely the one with the better judgment. He organized the soccer match putting all the insurgent leaders from various factions on the same team. The other team was made up of the traditional tribal leaders, many of whom had also been deeply at odds with each other. Now people who had literally been trying to kill each other were on the same team. Wati distributed the peace people between the two teams.

We went out to a raggedy vacant lot in Chiang Mai, set up markers for goals, and began to play. Within minutes we knew something profound was happening. Former enemies were working together for a common purpose. People who had hated each other were laughing as they helped each other up from stumbles. Reconciliation was not just a vague idea in the mist of a somewhat hoped-for future—it was suddenly a lived experience, and we were all delighting in it. Anger turned to

Author trying in vain to defend in the Naga reconciliation soccer match.

shouts of encouragement. Words of bitterness and accusation became laughter and cheers.

At halftime we sat in the grass planning how to take this experience back to Nagaland. My team won 4-2 on penalty kicks—no thanks to me but with deep appreciation for the Rev. V.K. Nuh, the "man of the match" who made 2 saves in goal though he was 80 years old! As we drove back to our venue for the talks everyone was making plans for the reconciliation football matches to be held in Nagaland.

Author showing how poor he is at heading a soccer ball.

The spirit of unity and working together for a common purpose continued in the talks. By the end of that four-day session, we arrived at the first common statement about reconciliation endorsed by all the major Naga insurgent factions.

Those matches planned in Chiang Mai were played back in Nagaland. One was held in Kohima, the capital of Nagaland. Another was held in Dimapur, the largest city. In each match, the Naga political groups formed one team. The other team was drawn from civil society groups who were part of the FNR. Before the match, there was a joint prayer meeting, and a choir drawn from cadres in all the factions sang together. The Dimapur match included a ceremony of widows and orphans of the men killed in the factional fighting, giving bouquets of flowers and offering words of forgiveness to all the members of the insurgent team.

Soccer became a peace game, opening up new relationships and helping people who had been at war sense in their flesh and bones what reconciliation was. They could be on a team together.

CHAPTER 29

The Impossible Walk

"BUT THAT'S IMPOSSIBLE!" said a number of participants of the conflict transformation workshop in Sierra Leone
as they dropped out of the training exercise.

The group had been given a challenge to walk about 10
yards in a line, keeping their ankles in touch with the ankles of
the people on either side of them in the line. If the line broke
anywhere they would all have to return to the starting point.
For 70 people to do this exercise together, it quickly became
evident that this seemingly simple task was actually a serious
challenge. After a number of efforts that disintegrated into
small groups trying to walk together, about 20 people drifted
off to the edges of the field and refused to participate. "That's
impossible," some said.

∾

Forging peace in a country shattered by war seems an
impossible task. How does reconciliation take place when
rebels have cut off the hands of civilians leaving a huge population of disabled people unable to earn their living in

conditions that are daunting to even the most able-bodied person? How does reconciliation take place when the bitterness is deep, corruption rife and fear still prevalent even though United Nations peacekeeping soldiers patrol the cities and countryside? Peace is impossible.

Daniel Hunter and I had been invited to Sierra Leone shortly after the end of the war to do conflict transformation and reconciliation workshops. We quickly noticed a pervasive passivity in the country. In 2004, Sierra Leone was rated #1 on the U.N.'s World

The ankle walk in Sierra Leone.

Misery Index. Over half of the Gross National Product (GNP) in the country was from international aid. When we began the training, we told people they were responsible for their learning and that they needed to choose to maximize their learning. Instead, we met resistance that insisted *we* were fully responsible for whatever might happen. We use experiential education methods that demand participation, so passivity was a guarantee that the training would be of minimal value.

Then we did the "ankle walk." In many training programs I speak of "peace games" as serving a similar pedagogical function as "war games" for the military. Through war games, various exercises and simulations, soldiers are trained to analyze situations they encounter. They learn to work together effectively and to employ new skills to accomplish their tasks. Peace games also teach people how to analyze situations they encounter, work together efficiently, and employ new skills to aid in accomplishing tasks. The tasks we have in mind, however, aim to turn conflict from a destructive and harmful experience into a positive, constructive experience. The ankle walk was a peace game that posed the challenge of dealing creatively with a task that seemed impossible.

So as the group of dropouts sat grumbling under a nearby tree, Daniel and I decided an intervention was necessary. Daniel, in a voice that could be heard by everyone, asked those still working on the task if they had noticed that some of their group had dropped out. They had. Daniel asked if they were interested in why their colleagues quit. They agreed to ask, which they then did. The dropouts responded that the task was impossible. Daniel then said, "No, it isn't. I saw 120 people successfully manage this challenge." The dropouts couldn't believe it, but Daniel assured them that others had succeeded in the task. He asked if they wanted to try again, and they agreed to re-enter the activity.

Workshop participants try to figure out how to walk together.

The full group then organized and began to strategize. They identified leaders who had ideas about how to coordinate their efforts. They experimented and learned from their mistakes, then tried again. Eventually, they successfully walked ankle-to-ankle in a line—all 70 of the participants. When they reached the finish line, they celebrated having accomplished a difficult challenge that they had earlier thought was impossible.

During the debriefing, we identified skills and actions they needed to succeed in the exercise. We looked at how those skills and actions would work in facing the difficult challenges of peace-building and reconciliation. Whereas at the beginning of the training most of the participants were passive, assuming that others needed to take the responsibility for making peace (U.N. or political figures), by the end of the training participants were accepting their own responsibility to be God's agents for reconciliation. Rather than saying reconciliation is impossible, or if it doesn't happen someone else is to blame, these men and women were excitedly and eagerly exploring and discussing the specific ways they could make a difference in schools and churches or in communities and the nation as a whole.

When we are faced with situations that seem impossible, how do we react? When we hear daunting and disheartening news, do we assume the situation is hopeless? Do we consign ourselves to passivity, guaranteeing that our prophecy of doom and gloom will be self-fulfilling?

Or do we realize that, throughout history, others have found the way to do the impossible? Do we nurture hope in ourselves? Do we find ways to work together, to experiment and learn from our mistakes? Do we keep our focus on the goal with determination that we can get there?

Jesus said, "*With God all things are possible*" (Mark 10:27). Faith in the belief that the impossible is possible can infuse us with energy to engage in the kind of action that takes us where nobody believed we could ever go.

CHAPTER 30

An Eggxercise in Unity

WHO WOULD GUESS that a humble chicken egg could play a role in creating a people's movement? But eggs became the symbol for building trust that assisted in the psychological turning point for the Nagas in northeast India.

Since 1947 the Nagas sought independence from India, and in the mid-1950s the struggle burst into an open war between the Nagas and the Indian army. Throughout a long history of flawed peace accords and splits among Naga groups, the agenda was determined by those with the guns—whether the Indian government or the Naga political groups. The grassroots people's organizations—the churches, the women's groups, the student groups, the human rights groups, and civic organizations—were on the sidelines raising their voices but being ignored.

In 1999, I was involved with these people's organizations in a series of workshops in Calcutta. Our goal was to develop a united movement to push for reconciliation among the Nagas and peace with India. Basically, we wanted to develop a peace constituency that was no longer at the margins but was a driving force.

The problem, however, was a lack of trust. The Nagas are made up of many different tribes and sub-tribes, and the Naga political factions fall roughly along some of those tribal lines. Many Naga community figures were assassinated by one faction or another, so even those in the grassroots organizations were worried

Participants at the Naga training and strategizing meetings in Calcutta.

about being betrayed by those of another tribe to the insurgent group closest to their competitors. Furthermore, Indian authorities would stir up differences to keep the Nagas disunited and weak. Unless the Naga community organizations could build effective bridges to each other bound with trust strong enough to resist Indian interference and Naga factionalism, there would be no hope of giving a transcendent message for reconciliation.

As the time neared to head to Calcutta, I thought about how to experientially connect to these Naga community leaders about trust. The idea of using raw eggs came to me beginning with the game of egg toss, where you have to work carefully with your partner for you both to succeed. The idea developed from there.

Early in the first Calcutta workshop, I had the leaders form into small working groups of four or five people. In those groups I distributed a raw egg to each person. I led a reflection on the egg as everyone held it in their hands. They could feel the weight of the egg, the heft of the yoke inside that fragile shell. We reflected on the life that was inside but that could be so easily destroyed by dropping the egg or smashing it with our hands. One mistake and all the potential for life in that amazing construction would be gone.

We continued to reflect on how our lives are like those eggs, like the egg in my hand. My life is wondrous and yet so fragile. One awful mistake and my life leaks out into nothingness. That egg is me. The egg in your hands is your life. My life is in my hands. Then I asked every person to give their egg to another person in the group.

Author receives a Naga shawl in appreciation for his peacemaking work with the Nagas.

For 24 hours, each person's egg would be in the care of someone else, someone from a different tribe, from a different organization. Our lives would be in others' hands.

The workshop went on with all kinds of exercises and activities. We moved chairs around from the large plenary group to small

Wati Aier speaks at the Naga training and strategizing sessions.

working groups and back again. We left for lunch and dinner. At the end of the day, people headed off to the various places where we were housed. Throughout each activity, each person tended to the egg that had been entrusted to them. Each person had to be mindful of where the egg was and how to protect it whether we were walking in the streets of Calcutta, eating at a restaurant or moving chairs around in our meeting hall. Everyone had to be aware and give care to the life that was entrusted to them.

After 24 hours we gathered back in the small groups. Not a single egg had been lost or broken. The women enjoyed the care of the eggs while the men were extremely nervous! I had everyone return the egg to the person who had given it to them and share expressions of gratitude for the tender safe-keeping provided.

We concluded by gathering the eggs together, breaking them all and cooking a wonderful omelet. Eating the eggs of our lives together was almost a Eucharistic moment—an Egg-charist? Somehow, in the tangibility of that "eggxercise," deep chords of trust began to be woven, chords that continued to grow in the days and months ahead.

Before long, a Naga people's movement had been bonded together that would take away the momentum from those with the guns and give it to those demanding peace. A simple moment, a symbol that speaks to our hearts with clarity, an action that captures the essence of our historic task can be the turning point in a struggle. Rosa Parks refused to get out of her seat on a bus. The Nagas took care of raw eggs for 24 hours. And history was changed.

CHAPTER 31

Where's Our Chicken?

IN THIS BOOK, the egg comes first—and then the chicken! As a traveler of many miles, I've seen the conflicts that erupt when flights are delayed due to weather or mechanical problems. Tempers get frayed. Angry customers with their travel plans disrupted accost gate agents who try to keep their patience. Sometimes peacemaking has to be exercised in the common conflicts of just getting from here to there.

Years ago, before I began my global peacemaking work, I was involved in an accidental but certainly serendipitous experience of travel conflict transformation. The experience showed the collaborative artistic dimensions of peacemaking.

Sharon and I lived in Boston, and I wanted to visit my mother in Chicago. So I took Amtrak, and, with a backpack and guitar, boarded the train. It was an uneventful trip until the station after Cleveland. We were informed that a freight train ahead of us had derailed, forcing us to make a major detour.

The train sat awhile and then slowly backed up all the way to Cleveland. We were shunted onto side tracks that took us way off the main line into the Ohio farmland. At times, the tracks were in deplorable shape, so our express train had to creep along with occasional long stops in the middle of nowhere and no explanation from the train crew. We were due into Chicago at 1 p.m., but that time found us eating unplanned lunches in the dining car.

Somewhere in the middle of the afternoon someone noticed my guitar up in the overhead luggage rack. He said in a stage whisper, "If this was the movies, someone would break out a guitar, and we'd all start singing." I took the hint and asked the people in the car if they'd like a folk music singalong. The response was enthusiastic—we'd all been bored and disgusted, so music was a most welcome distraction. I pulled out my guitar and started to play. If people knew the song, they'd all join in. "Puff the Magic Dragon" filled the car. If nobody knew the song, I'd do it solo. With lots of laughter, singing and applause we continued for about an hour until my fingers could take it no more.

Late in the afternoon we finally got back to the main line. As we rolled toward Elkhart, Indiana, rumors came down the car that we could all get Kentucky Fried Chicken. Sure enough, as we pulled into the station, we saw luggage dollies piled high with boxes of Kentucky Fried Chicken. They started serving from the rear of the train. I was sitting in the front half of the first car. They ran out of chicken halfway through our car.

I could smell the aroma of freshly fried chicken wafting from the rear as the conductor came to us. He sheepishly apologized, saying they miscounted the number of passengers. The dining car had been cleaned out from the unexpected lunch, but they did have a few burritos, a couple containers of yogurt, some M&Ms and other odd items that we were welcome to. So I had a bag of plain M&Ms for my dinner.

This is ridiculous, I thought. So I whipped out my ticket envelope and began writing a ballad to commemorate the day's events. I wrote three verses and a chorus. The last line stumped me. I just couldn't come up with a good ending to the chorus, but time was wasting. It's now or never, I thought.

I stood up and told my car mates that I'd written a ballad about our experiences. They roared with excitement and urged me on. So I began to sing:

We started out clickety-clack
Chicago-bound on a fast Amtrak
Then Murphy's Law was applied
And our day began its downhill slide.

So tell me, where's our chicken?
Where's our chicken?
Where's our chicken?
We're anxious to be fed.

We took a jaunt down south a bit
An Ohio heartland scenic route trip
Saw lot of towns didn't want to see
Been to lot of places didn't want to be

So tell me, where's our chicken? ...

Time drags on as we creep on down the line
What does it take to get this baby flyin'?
We've hung in tough 'cause there ain't much else to do,
Perhaps with some humor we'll see it all through.

So tell me, where's our chicken? ...

The car exploded in applause. "***Do it again!***" I sang it again. Then they wanted it a third time. This time the entire car joined raucously in on the chorus.

Suddenly the conductor walked in just as the entire car full of passengers was singing, "Where's our chicken?" He smiled, shook his head, turned around and walked out.

As the train continued rapidly toward Chicago, people in the car animatedly talked to one another. Someone said, "Amtrak should make a commercial about us—even when things go bad you can have a great time riding Amtrak!"

We finally pulled into Chicago, eight hours late. Many people had missed connections, and Amtrak offered to put people up in hotels. As we got off the train, I could hear the snarls and anger from the passengers in the cars behind us. But as folks got off our car, they were laughing and shaking hands in fond farewell.

All of us on that Amtrak train experienced the same delay, but the atmosphere in our car was radically different from the rest of the train. All it took to transform the situation was someone willing to speak up with a fresh idea, someone willing to respond and people willing to join in with their own positive energy. Rather than letting their experience be dictated by what was out of their control, we used our own power to act within the situation. We couldn't change the time the train arrived in Chicago, but we could take charge of the atmosphere in the car and how we would feel as we got off that train. Those are the decision moments that transform conflicts from negative experiences to positive experiences.

CHAPTER 32

"This Is New for Us"

"THIS IS NEW for us," the Naga factional leader said.

We were at reconciliation talks in Thailand with Nagas from different factions. Nagas in the northeast of India struggled for independence for over 60 years. Around 1980, the first of many splits developed among the Nagas. This led to levels of violence rivaling the military conflict between the Indian army and Naga insurgents. Beginning in 2008, a series of reconciliation meetings were held at Chiang Mai, Thailand over a number of years. I attended many of those meetings, playing a role in the international mediation facilitation team.

Most of the Nagas are Baptists, including the insurgents. Worship was part of the Chiang Mai process, including opening worship services and a Sunday service if the talks went over the weekend. I was asked to preach a Sunday service.

I selected one of my favorite peacemaking texts: *"Do not be overcome by evil, but overcome evil with good"* (Romans 12:21). I preached how we can be overcome by evil from within because we let the wrong done by our enemy be the excuse to justify our own evil. But God calls us to a different way, using good means to strike at the heart of the spirit of evil. Such action can even bring our enemies to repentance. Evil is overcome by good.

After the service, we took up the negotiation process with the mediation team meeting separately with each of the factions. In one group, the leader began by saying he intended to start the session by giving us a list of all the people murdered under the orders of the leader of one of the other groups. I've received many such lists in my time working with the Nagas with each group accusing the other group of numerous atrocities and betrayals. But then the leader said that listening to the sermon prompted him to take a different approach. He didn't give us the list. Instead, he said he would look to the future and how we might find some positive steps to continue the reconciliation process. Our whole session was more positive thanks to this leader interacting thoughtfully with the biblical teaching. He made a conscious and deliberate choice to conduct his affairs in a different way.

Author with leaders from opposing Naga insurgent factions.

As the session wore on, this Naga leader began slipping back into old familiar habits of thinking and speaking. One of the other factions had taken a provocative action, and so this leader angrily said that his group just had to respond in a certain negative way, a way that would escalate the situation.

I quickly challenged him. He didn't "have to" act in any particular way. Acting in such a reactionary fashion gave all the power for determining what would happen to the other side. I challenged him that God gives us the freedom to act creatively, even generously. We can choose to act by a different script than the old, tired, dead-end conflict script we've worked with for so long and so fruitlessly.

I gave a quick brainstorm list of many other actions that could be taken just as easily. They would be actions that would not compromise his side's own convictions, but that also weren't determined by the provocative actions of the other group. Some of the options could open up opportunities to further the reconciliation process. He could take creative actions that would put the other side in a difficult situation where they would have to act positively or they would lose credibility with the Naga public.

The leader listened carefully to what I was saying then responded, "This is new for us." But he took the ideas to heart. Like someone trying on a new shoe, he didn't just take it off. He tried it, walked around a bit. He liked the size and feel. He decided to keep walking with this new way of thinking.

Peacemaking is often the work of inner liberation. Our minds need to be freed from the determinism of conflicted cycles of reaction. We let what we do be conditioned by what our enemy does. We surrender our power of self-determination to the other. Then we become bound to them by a chain of reactivity, jerking each other around.

Peace requires that we set ourselves free from that chain. We need to take our own cues for action from what is good, specifically the good that is rooted in God rather than the evil that binds our enemies and us in never-ending cycles of ever-deeper hurt. Once we choose the freedom to act in what is good, divine surprises can unfold—even in the midst of our conflicts.

Yes, it is a new way of thinking for most of us. Freedom begins in our minds, choosing to become masters of our own wills, and then choosing what is good.

PART 8

Special Days

In my travels, I've stumbled onto many special days. I've celebrated the independence days of many nations on their various dates. I've celebrated Easter twice in the same year, in China and in the Republic of Georgia because of different Christian calendars. Two days became extra-special because of the experiences that grew out of them.

CHAPTER 33

The Best Labor Day Ever

THERE I WAS, stooping low and swinging a machete at the weeds around a small palm tree. I was surrounded by 50 or 60 other people "chopping bush" with machetes, raking the weeds and trash, loading wheelbarrows to haul it all to dumpsters, or sweeping the sidewalks and parking lots.

It was Labor Day in Jamaica, a national holiday established in the 1970s as a time for people to join together in labor to benefit their communities. Most churches participated in various community projects. I had joined with the Denham Town Baptist Church because they were at the center of their community clean up, and Denham Town needed a lot of cleaning up!

Denham Town is a neighborhood of Kingston, Jamaica's capital city. Over the last 15 years or so, Denham Town was swept up in the roaring tides of political and criminal violence that produced one of the highest murder rates for any country in the world. A few years earlier, the political gangs were so rampant that Denham Town was like a war zone with open gun battles in the streets. Many people left. Churches closed. One church was burned to the ground. But Denham Town Baptist Church stayed. They maintained their ministries in the community, gaining respect even in the midst of all the street fighting. The church building was never shot up. The fighting now isn't as intense as it was, but the gangs and the violence continue.

On the Tuesday night one week before Labor Day, I went to the church to lead sessions on Bible-based conflict transformation. To get onto the street where the church building was, we talked with men who erected a barricade of scrap wood and metal across the street. When they heard we were going to the church, they opened up enough of a hole that we could drive through.

Author "chopping bush."

After the training session, I talked to one of the men at the barricade to hear what was behind their actions. He said that it was to keep police and outsiders away, as they have often caused problems in the community. I knew I was getting only one perspective on the situation because the gangs manning the barricades were also part of the problem.

While I was in Jamaica on that particular trip, Amnesty International released a report stating that in 2006, Jamaican police allegedly killed 138 people. The report detailed the problems of police abuse and lack of accountability. Whatever the full story, it was clear that the whole community of Denham Town felt marginalized. They were supporters of the opposing political party and perceived that the police who answered to the government were against them.

How do you clean up a neighborhood not just from weeds and dirt but also from violence and despair? The brothers and sisters at Denham Town Baptist Church have been working on that challenge for many long years. The church organized a soccer league for young men in the community. They visit the homes nearby, getting to know their neighbors and their neighbors' needs. I admire their courage and persistence. They have not been intimidated by the violence around them, but rather have responded with love and creativity.

On Labor Day, they were at the center of the community clean up, providing tools and giving directions. Sidney, one of the church lay-leaders, coordinated all the efforts. He drew in the young men drinking rum as they sat under a palm tree alongside the elderly churchwomen. The church arranged for a

Community lunch after a hard day of labor.

water truck to come and fill up a pool for kids to play in, right in the middle of an intersection.

When everyone had labored side-by-side for about three hours, we could see a huge difference in the streets, yards and lots. Church members brought pews out from the sanctuary into the parking lot. They placed a piece of plywood across the top, and then brought out countless boxes of chicken with rice and beans. Sidney asked me to say a word to the community, so I spoke about the great work they had done in coming together to make their community better. It was a bit of the Kingdom of God come to Denham Town. But every day can be Labor Day if everyone will work together to make the community a better place. We blessed the food and ate together—church members and gang members, young and old, men and women, boys and girls. It felt wondrously like the feeding of the 5,000 in the Bible.

Author enjoying lunch after morning's hard work.

After lunch, Sidney brought me over to meet a young man. He was in a gang, but he called a church prayer line for help in getting out of a life of crime and violence. He admitted to being a part of various robberies and shootings, but he wanted a new life. Sidney introduced him to some of the young men in the church, and they gathered around him and prayed with him. He was one life, one young person taking a small step in a new direction. He was met with the encouragement and support he would need to make that journey. He knew where to turn because the members of Denham Town Baptist Church weren't hiding in their sanctuary—they were in the streets of the community.

A devastated, violence-wracked neighborhood is being cleaned up. The tools, I believe, used by God for the cleanup are men and women willing to go out and get dirty. They know their neighborhood. They meet people and love them. They overcome evil with soccer balls and machetes, with labor and prayer, with words of welcome and words of encouragement. Community transformation doesn't happen without people willing to risk getting out where life is gritty and dangerous to make a difference. That's what they were doing in Denham Town.

CHAPTER 34

A Birthday Surprise

I WAS ALONE for by birthday, far, far from home. I was in Myanmar with a day off from a heavy work schedule. It was raining outside, and inside my small hotel room without internet had become claustrophobic. What seemed to be my most pathetic birthday ever was about to become one of the most memorable.

It was over a year after the so-called "Saffron Revolution," when Burmese Buddhist monks participated in one of the waves of a nonviolent protest against the repression of the military government. Many monks were killed, others arrested. Their actions made worldwide news.

I was teaching conflict transformation and had a very full schedule except for one day. That day off fell on my birthday. I didn't let anybody know it was my birthday. At first, I cherished the quiet moments in my hotel room. It was a rainy, dreary day, so I relaxed and read most of the morning.

In the afternoon, boredom took over. I decided I needed to get out in spite of the rain and get some exercise. The Shwedagon Pagoda was a moderate walk from my hotel. The pagoda is Myanmar's iconic landmark, an astounding temple complex with a massive golden stupa surrounded by many smaller stupas, alcoves, side chapels and stairs coming up the hill from the four cardinal directions. I'd been there many times before and thought it would be a refreshing afternoon treat to wander there. The rain was letting up, so I headed out.

I planned to sit in one of the cool breezeways to reflect, read and perhaps write. I left my shoes at the bottom of the steps as did all the other worshippers and visitors. I padded up the marble stairs in bare feet. At the top, some of the marble was still wet from the rain, so I used an ice-skating motion to keep my balance on the slick surface.

When the rains started pelting down again I ducked into a beautiful, sheltered spot. I had only been sitting a few moments when a young monk in

Author with a Buddhist monk at Shwedagon Pagoda.

a maroon robe came up to me. I invited him to join me, and we began to talk. It was a delightful time. We talked about where I was from and about the pagoda. (He often gave tours to English-speaking visitors, a free service from the monks.)

He told me about the huge bell in the structure where we sat; it had sunk into the river while being ferried to Yangon during the Anglo-Burmese War and had been retrieved after independence in 1948. I had a peace button given to me by a friend, one of a number he gave me to distribute on my travels. I gave it to him and talked about my teaching about making peace.

After a bit, we were joined by a friend of his—another young man dressed in regular street garb. His English was a bit better; he taught English to the monks. He used to be a monk himself. They began to tell me about the pagoda as a religious place and about the Buddhist beliefs and practices. It helped that I knew quite a bit about Buddhism, so I could understand their English even with their heavy accents. As I shared about peacemaking work, they quickly cut me off saying, "We don't talk about politics here." *Hmmm. Monks had been gunned down in the streets not too long ago.* I wasn't sure what all this meant, but obviously talking politics was more risky than walking with bare feet on wet marble.

When the rain let up, they took me to some of the sights in the complex and told me about the meaning of numbers in Buddhism. "Nine" is the number for Buddha, "7" the number for the world, and "3" the number for your father, mother and teachers. Since it was my birthday, everything was special. They showed me the practices of pouring water related to the day of your birth.

They invited me to meditate with them. We chatted about Christian and Buddhist meditation practices—the similarities and differences. They guided me to a side chapel where people were meditating. We sat together for a long while in silence.

When we finished meditating, we walked toward the center of the Shwedagon complex. After a bit the rain started pelting down. The winds swept the rain under the roof, driving us deeper into the shelter. We'd been together for about two hours. Huddling close in the wet chill, suddenly they started talking politics.

They were from the Rakhine (Arakan) State in the southwest of Myanmar near Bangladesh. Rakhine State is one of the poorest areas in the country and a place where the military has engaged in a lot of repression. These two men had been involved in the demonstrations when they were both monks. They told about the soldiers invading their monastery and how they ran away. They shared about many monks being gunned down. They shared about friends being arrested and tortured. One left the monastery and returned to lay life. But both had maintained their activism.

They were very excited about my work. We had a lot of fun practicing English as we talked in great detail about the practice of nonviolence. Our huddle under the shelter in Shwedagon became a most holy place. As we finally said our goodbyes late in the day. I told them our meeting was a divine appointment.

What a birthday gift! Sometimes in places of stifling fear, the gift of trust needs to be carefully unwrapped with compassionate and patient listening. Layers of protection are slowly peeled away as trust and friendship is built. Finally, you can hold the treasure that is more precious than a diamond—the trust of another. It was a very happy birthday.

Reprise

PEACEMAKING ISN'T JUST a matter for trained people with the proper degrees and credentials. Otherwise, I would have done nothing. Peacemaking isn't just for the hard-core activists—that may be me. I've learned so much from ordinary people trying to live ordinary lives who acted in extraordinary ways in times of crisis. Peacemaking is for all of us.

We can add fuel to the fires of our conflicts, or we can act creatively and courageously in ways that will open up new possibilities full of hope. Our stages for peacemaking may be different—a family, a congregation, a community group, a local neighborhood, a nation or the family of nations.

Philip Kakungulu at a human rights rally in Uganda.

Let me bring Philip Kakungulu back into the story, this time using mostly his words: "My entire life I have always been intrigued by Ephesians 6:15, '*The feet shod with the Gospel of Peace.*' In the process of putting on the Armor of God, it's not surprising that feet are the last part of the body that are clothed. No one begins to dress from the feet upwards."

After a time of great frustration, Philip got the invitation to participate in the 10-day Training of Conflict Transformation Trainers in Kenya. He described it as "a freshness of life blowing over my life." Then, on the last day: "Rev. Daniel took out a safari case. We all were puzzled at what this might mean. He got out pairs of old socks, and he asked us to pick out one pair each. I took my time, and it instantly hit me that this was no charity concert. The man was actually passing down an impartation of the anointing to travel into places of brokenness with the Gospel of Peace. I guess some of the participants might have thought: Is this the best gift that this American reverend can give to us? That pair of socks which I received and I now own was actually my turning point."

Philip goes on to say: "I have moved on since then with this pair of socks, into marginalized communities, preaching peace and running for hope. With my socks, I have participated in freedom walks in some of the most dangerous places and environments in Africa. There is no doubt this pair of socks is steadily leading the race to the shores of hope where humanity can anticipate to arrive. I then believe that God is always hovering over

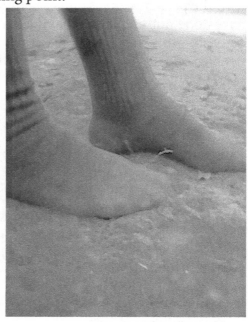

Philip sports his peace socks.

the turbulent sea of life in Africa and beyond … using lay people like me to make known his Grace. With this pair of socks,

I am persuaded that I can arrive where God is vital, where humanity dreams of arriving, in a place called Peace."

Philip's personal journey turned around because he took the strange gift of socks seriously. With those socks he has now "run" long distances.

Dorothy Day is one of my peacemaking heroes. She said, "People say, what is the sense of our small effort? They cannot see that we must lay one brick at a time, take one step at a time." One step at a time—that is the only place we can begin. That is the only way to continue.

I can only wear one pair of socks at a time—OK, if it's cold I might wear two, but no more. Friend, whether you know it or not, you are the socks. We are all the socks, God's gift to cover the pains and wounds of a hurting world. The world only needs us to be who we are in what is at hand for each of us to do well today. Do the work of peace one step at a time. Be the socks that only you can be. The words may not scroll through your mind as they did mine, but they can scroll across the page: You are the socks! We are the socks! Peace be upon us all in our journey, one step at a time!

Our Story

Since 2007, ReadTheSpirit Books has been publishing authors with a purpose: to improve our world, one story at a time. Media means connection. We often say: Good media builds good community.

We believe that our readers—men and women just like you, all around the world—are a part of this larger effort to connect lives through the stories we tell. You can help by simply telling friends about this book and encouraging them to start reading. Most of our books are designed for individual reading—and also for small-group discussion. So, please consider inviting friends to discuss this book with you.

We always appreciate hearing from readers like you. Want to thank the author? Ask a question? Suggest an idea? Find out about author appearances? Just email us at ReadTheSpirit@gmail.com

The book you are holding is part of a larger collection of books by writers that encourage peacemaking, celebrate diversity, strengthen caregivers, rebuild impoverished communities, train the next generation of leaders and, most importantly, inspire each of us to enjoy a better day.

Please, take a moment to look at some of the other ReadTheSpirit books you may enjoy reading. Your next inspiration is just a book away.

Related Books

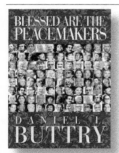

Blessed Are the Peacemakers
Daniel L. Buttry, 2011

In the pages of this book, you will meet more than 100 heroes, but most of them are not the kind of heroes our culture celebrates for muscle, beauty and wealth. These are peacemakers. Watch out! Reading about their lives may inspire you to step up into their courageous circle.

www.InterfaithPeacemakers.com

ISBN: 978-1-934879-23-8

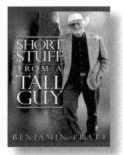

Interfaith Heroes 1 & 2
Daniel L. Buttry, 2008

These two volumes profile more than 70 interfaith heroes, spiritual leaders and peacemakers throughout time and across the globe. These courageous men and women crossed traditional boundaries of religious groups to build stronger communities.

www.InterfaithPeacemakers.com

ISBN: 978-1-934879-00-9

Short Stuff From A Tall Guy
Benjamin Pratt, 2015

For the first time in book form, author and counselor Benjamin Pratt collects dozens of his true-life stories that invites readers on a spiritual journey marked by compassion, humor and honesty about dilemmas, doubts and challenges that men and women face everyday.

www.ShortStuffFromATallGuy.com

ISBN: 978-1-939880-90-1

United America
Wayne Baker, 2014

Dr. Wayne Baker reports on a surprising truth about Americans: We are united by 10 Core Values. This truth is empowering because it enables us to rise above and see beyond political polarization, Washington gridlock, and the rhetoric of culture wars and class warfare.

www.UnitedAmericaBook.com

ISBN: 978-1-939880-29-1

Print and ebooks available on Amazon.com and other retailers.

CPSIA information can be obtained
at www.ICGtesting.com
Printed in the USA
FFHW020550240120
58029610-63158FF